Strategies for Success

Hilary Barnard is a consultant specialising in strategic planning and managing organisational change in voluntary and arts organisations. As council for voluntary service general secretary in Newham and as a trustee of several charities, he has wide experience of helping voluntary organisations with their planning. He has been a tutor on the Open University Business School programme on Managing Voluntary and Non-profit Enterprises.

Perry Walker developed his interest in strategic planning when in the Civil Service. He attended the Corporate Planning in Practice course at the Henley Management Centre and helped his department to produce its first corporate plan. He pursued this interest when working for the John Lewis Partnership, particularly in the strategic evaluation of personnel activities. Since 1989 he has been chair of the New Economics Foundation, to which he introduced strategic planning. He is a member of the Strategic Planning Society.

NCVO – voice of the voluntary sector

NCVO champions the cause of the
voluntary sector. It believes that the
voluntary sector enriches society and
needs to be promoted and supported. It
works to improve its effectiveness,
identify unmet needs and encourage
initiative to meet them.

Established in 1919 as the
representative body for the voluntary
sector in England, NCVO now gives
voice to some 600 national organisations
– from large 'household name' charities
to small self-help groups involved in all
areas of voluntary and social action. It is
also in touch with thousands of other
voluntary bodies and groups, and has
close links with government departments,
local authorities, institutions of the
European Union and the business sector.

Strategies for Success

A Self-Help Guide
to Strategic Planning
for Voluntary
Organisations

Hilary Barnard and
Perry Walker

 NCVO Publications

Published by NCVO Publications

(incorporating Bedford Square Press)

imprint of the National Council for Voluntary Organisations

Regent's Wharf, 8 All Saints Street, London N1 9RL

First published 1994

Typeset by James Jenkins Typesetting

Printed in Great Britain by The Lavenham Press, Suffolk

A catalogue record for this book is available from the British Library.

ISBN 0 7199 1414 0

Contents

Contents

Exercises

Figures and Tables

Acknowledgements

We would like to thank the following people for their help in preparing this book:

As critical readers – Brenda Allan, Sue Beardon, Roger Booker, Enrico Carpanini, John Horner, Harbinder Kaur, Alan Lawton, John Lock, Sue Nelson, David McKevitt, Sheelagh Stewart, Jan Tallis, Carolyn White and Robin Wilkinson.

For making their time and much information available so that we could develop case study material – Michael Archer, Doug Bourne, Martin Bradshaw, Robert Davies, Martin Eede, Marion Fitzpatrick, Bevis Gillett, Colin Logan, Foster Murphy, Philippa Tristram, Bernadette Vallely and Bev Walters.

We would like to acknowledge the help and ideas of the tutors and students of the Open University Business School course on strategic management.

We should also like to acknowledge the financial support which was kindly supplied by Marks & Spencer. Finally we acknowledge also the support of NCVO itself, particularly Tim Dartington and Jackie Sallon, our editor, whose patience we have tried but never broken.

Introduction

Let our advance worrying become our advance thinking and planning.
Winston Churchill

This introduction explains why we have written this book, who it is for, and what you can expect to gain through using it.

The pressure for strategy

Strategy is concerned with understanding where you are now, what it is your organisation wants to achieve over time, and how it will achieve it. So strategy is thus closely connected to the pursuit of success, however you choose to define success for your organisation.

Voluntary organisations will have many of their own reasons for developing strategies – reviewing traditional areas of work, looking for new activities or funding, ensuring the best use of staff and volunteers, and so on. In recent years, however, much of the pressure on voluntary organisations to develop strategy has come from external sources.

Some of these outside forces are easy to identify – community care, the pursuit of European Union funding, making an effective contribution to inner city regeneration, and the desire to sustain the environment. Changes even closer to some organisations are also forcing the pace on longer-term planning, notably the contract culture and the growth of service agreements.

Nevertheless, even if the pressure is coming from the outside, the process need not be approached reactively or cynically. The process of developing and implementing strategy should be positive and enriching for all concerned.

Pressure to develop a strategy can be met by:

- ignoring it and hoping it will go away
- doing whatever is necessary to counteract it
- taking the challenge and running with it
- anticipating the challenge and helping to shape it

If you choose one of the last two options, you will need to take some time to consider future directions for your organisation. This will often involve major changes in ways of working and break new ground for the organisation.

The words 'strategic planning' convey to some people a degree of complexity that can be forbidding. In a number of voluntary organisations, large, medium and even small, there has been a tendency to hand the process over to consultants. It is left to them to organise, document and effectively control the strategy. We believe that in these circumstances the organisation does not really 'own' its strategy, and this may lead to problems. However, the question of where consultants may add value to the development of an organisation's strategy is considered in Chapter 2.

Our philosophy

The philosophy of this book is one of self-help. It draws on the traditions of mutual and communal self-help in the voluntary sector. It is our experience and that of NCVO that there is a gap in advice tailored to voluntary organisations doing their own strategic planning. We have simplified the process of strategic planning for voluntary organisations to make self-help feasible, particularly for smaller and medium-sized organisations. Any planning activities that your organisation already pursues can be incorporated into the process we describe. The process requires organisations to be honest, to face the possibility of painful change, and to commit a lot of time and energy.

The book sets out a complete process for strategic planning, and we recommend that you scan the whole book first to gain an overview of its content. Within the overall process, we offer a choice of methods wherever possible, although we have not tried to be exhaustive.

We know that many organisations will want to adapt our process and techniques. However, there are some circumstances where there is just one way to do it. Perhaps the best way to describe the book is to say that we offer a set meal with some choices and not an à la carte menu!

The book represents a snapshot of the development of strategic planning in the voluntary sector. We would welcome feedback from readers on which aspects they have found most helpful, and there is a form for your comments on page 201 The dialogue will advance the understanding and application of strategic planning methods in the voluntary sector.

The language of strategy

An overtechnical approach to developing strategy puts many people off and means that they do not participate effectively. This runs counter to the emphasis in the voluntary sector on empowerment. We share the aspiration of many in the voluntary sector to involve trustees and volunteers in strategic planning.

It is one of our objectives in this book to demystify the language of strategy and to keep our explanations as simple as possible. We will be delighted if as a result of reading it you feel more confident about using the words and concepts that fit your organisation.

The origins of the language of strategic planning lie partly in warfare and partly in the business world. There are many things that distinguish the voluntary sector from these two environments. They include:

- values
- diverse sources of influence
- range and methods of involvement
- the 'gift relationship' – based on altruism and co-operation – between users, volunteers and the organisation
- role of funders
- multiple sources of funding

Nevertheless, voluntary organisations can benefit and borrow from the experience of other sectors without losing this distinctiveness.

Who this book is for

Our audience is those people who want to develop an effective strategic planning process that will enable their voluntary or other non-profit-making organisation to design and implement effective strategies. The book is therefore aimed at people and organisations who:

- are approaching strategic planning for the first time;
- want to add to their skills in this area;
- are participating in the process as well as designing it;
- want a refresher or reference book.

This is a book for trustees as much as for staff. The people who govern a charity may be referred to as trustees, management committee members, members of the committee, council members, executive committee members, or something similar. In this book we call them 'trustees' and refer to the committee or council on which they sit as the 'board of trustees'. They have a vital role as guardians of the organisation's purpose and have much to contribute to strategy. The book should also be useful for those approaching strategic planning in non-hierarchical organisations within the voluntary sector. We have not written it primarily for experienced strategic planners, but the book should help them to communicate their knowledge and expertise more widely.

We also take the view that the book is largely applicable to other non-profit-making organisations who consider themselves to be outside the voluntary sector. It will be apparent to members of such organisations where the approach does not fit. We hope that it will also prove relevant to readers who have an interest in voluntary organisations but are themselves from outside the voluntary sector, whether from the private or public sectors.

The core of our audience is made up of actual or potential 'voluntary sector planners'. The voluntary sector planner is someone within the sector who develops knowledge of and experience in planning. Voluntary sector planners are unlikely to be spending all their time on planning. This would imply that they were doing too much of the planning and too little management or management-level work to be effective. They should be enablers as much as technicians, concerned to identify good practice from outside the voluntary sector and combine it with insights from within the sector.

A workbook

This book is a workbook that has been designed for the active reader. It is intended to be read and used in the office, at board meetings or conferences, or at home.

Our approach has been influenced by the ideas of self-managed learning. Throughout the book, we have included exercises to help clarify and develop your understanding of strategic planning. Each exercise contains questions for you to answer. Many of the exercises can be done on a group basis but however you use the book, it is worth writing down your answers and keeping them, perhaps in a notebook.

In some cases by completing the exercise you will have accomplished that particular step of the strategy. The action points at the end of each chapter have also been designed to assist your review and use of material and to highlight a practical programme of action.

Most exercises will produce answers distinctive to your organisation which will be invaluable for pulling together your organisation's strategy. The book with your answers should be an essential reference tool when you are implementing your strategy.

This book relates all aspects of strategic planning to voluntary organisations, even if we have not always been able to use voluntary sector examples. However, it is not a general text on strategy. Books and articles which we believe you will find useful for further reference are listed in Appendix 4.

It will be helpful to use this book alongside the others in the series of NCVO Management Guides – Gawlinski and Graessle's *Planning Together*, which focuses on team work, Martin and Smith's *Planning for the Future,* which concentrates on business planning, and *Equality in Action* which concentrates on implementing equal opportunities.

The headlines

Each of the eight chapters of the book covers part of the sequence in the development of strategy:

- *Chapter 1* introduces the different notions of strategic planning.
- *Chapter 2* describes the process of strategic planning and recommends a process for voluntary organisations.
- *Chapter 3* shows you how to analyse your organisation's current position.
- *Chapter 4* illustrates ways to identify your organisation's sense of purpose.
- *Chapter 5* identifies how to formulate your organisation's strategy.
- *Chapter 6* examines the capability of your organisation to deliver your strategy.
- *Chapter 7* is about putting your organisation's chosen strategy into effect.
- *Chapter 8* enables you to review and learn from your experience of strategic planning.

Chapter 1
What is Strategic Planning?

We trained hard . . . but it seemed that every time we were beginning to form up into teams, we would be reorganised. I was to learn later in life that we tend to meet any new situation by reorganising and a wonderful method it can be for creating the illusion of progress while producing confusion, inefficiency and demoralisation.

Petronius Arbiter, 210 BC

This chapter is in two parts. The first part offers some definitions of strategic planning. The second part provides an outline of the benefits of planning, and how they have shifted over time.

Defining strategic planning

The quotation from Petronius Arbiter illustrates how unsatisfactory change for change's sake can be. It also highlights how continual restructuring does not produce success by itself. The fact that you are reading this book suggests that you are already exploring the case for a longer-term perspective for your organisation. In the process, you may already have encountered a range of somewhat confusing terms for strategy. This section offers some explanations.

'Strategic planning' is often seen as focusing on the harder aspects of strategy, covering services, products and markets, in contrast to 'strategic management' which emphasises the softer, people side of strategy and includes the role of management in strategy, the importance of organisation and style, and the contribution of managers to the implementation and control of strategy. We will embrace all these concerns within our use of the term 'strategic planning', and will go well beyond the common representation of a strategic plan as a document.

One definition of strategic planning is that it is a plan describing how an organisation interacts with its environment and changes internally to achieve its purpose. An interesting twist for a voluntary organisation is that this could even be the plan of how it will make itself redundant over a number of years.

The two leading UK texts on strategy adopt similar definitions. Cliff Bowman and David Asch focus on matching internal and external factors: 'the match an organisation makes between its own resources and the threats or risks and opportunities created by the external environment in which it operates.'

The definition adopted by Gerry Johnson and Kevan Scholes is on the same lines: 'the direction and scope of an organisation over the long term: ideally, which matches its resources to its changing environment, and in particular its markets, customers, or clients so as to meet stakeholder expectations.'

Following Johnson and Scholes, we would identify three components of strategic planning:

1 *Strategic analysis* where managers seek to understand the organisation's strategic options.

2 *Strategic choice* which is concerned with choosing between possible courses of action.

3 *Strategy implementation* which is about putting a chosen course of action into effect.

Looping the loop

It is the scale and complexity of these three tasks that causes strategic planning to be referred to as an iterative process. An iterative process is one that involves going through the same or a similar sequence of actions more than once. This is usually done at an increasing level of sophistication. So strategic planning is a continual process that does not progress neatly in a straight line from start to finish or have fixed and separate stages.

Other views of strategy

There are alternative views of strategy that are less traditional than those given above. Henry Mintzberg, a leading writer on organisational strategy and change, offers three other views of strategy:

1 *Strategy as pattern* – consistency of behaviour whether intended or not. It is the observable expression of the pattern that defines the strategy, often retrospectively. For a voluntary organisation, this strategy could be expressed in a pricing policy which defines who it wants and does not want to be users of its services. This form of strategy tends to be internally focused.
2 *Strategy as position* – a means of identifying where an organisation stands in the world. This could be in terms of the collaborative relationships that it seeks and then maintains with other voluntary organisations or the relationship it seeks with government. Voluntary organisations are sometimes highly competitive in their attempts to obtain the attention of a minister.
3 *Strategy as perspective* – an ingrained way of perceiving the world. Many value-based organisations may have such strategies whether they recognise them to be so or not. For example, the New Economics Foundation started out with the perspective that its relations with central government would be confrontational.

Exercise 1 A Presentation on Strategy

You have been asked to explain the concept of strategy to your board of trustees (or the equivalent group in your organisation), or senior managers.

Choose a definition that you feel comfortable with from those we have given above. Prepare a five-minute presentation which explains what you understand strategy to be.

To do the above exercise you will have chosen an approach that you feel suits your organisation and the context in which it is working. A simple view of strategy that you might have offered as a starting point is that strategy is where you want to go and how you are going to get there.

Deliberate and emergent strategies

A deliberate strategy is one that is precisely formulated with the intention of matching purpose, methods and outcomes to produce a written plan. Many organisations do not have this kind of strategy, for a variety of reasons. However, Henry Mintzberg suggests that every organisation has a strategy but it is not necessarily a deliberate one. Strategies range from a finely crafted heavyweight document at one extreme to a loose conception of organisational direction in the head of a staff member or volunteer at the other. Strategies that are not deliberate are called 'emergent'. This is because they emerge from the activities of the organisation. Here are two examples of emergent strategies.

Examples – deliberate and emergent strategies

NFB
The National Film Board (NFB) of Canada is a not-for-profit organisation. It established its early reputation in the

production of animated films and short documentaries. In the process, it funded one film maker whose film turned out to be much longer than expected. To distribute it the National Film Board turned to cinemas, and so accidentally learnt how to market feature-length films. Other film makers made use of this expertise and the NFB found itself pursing a revised strategy based on longer films.

Honda

Honda's first attempt to sell motorbikes in the US was a disaster. The bikes, large and powerful imitations of US machines, were too fragile for the rough handling that they received. In addition the five-person Japanese sales force arrived in the US just after the annual motorbike buying season had ended.

To understand their market better, the sales force travelled around on Honda minibikes. These were so much admired by dealers and potential bike purchasers that Honda's senior managers found it had rapidly acquired a distribution network and demand for a product that it had not originally intended to sell in the US market. Sales only then began to be developed with careful planning.

The success of emergent strategies depends on:

- *the significance of the development* – this was the case in both examples;
- *leadership response and intentions* – Honda's senior managers were able to take the opportunity to sell the minibikes;
- *the nature of and opportunities for change* – the NFB learnt how to market feature-length films.

Emergent strategies can develop untended and take root in many different places in the organisation, even if they are not initially taken note of. This process of strategy proliferation may be conscious or unconscious. If conscious, it may be managed, but this need not always be the case. New strategic themes can emerge, particularly in periods of change where there is scope for experimentation or renewal.

Example – emergent and deliberate strategy

Morley College

Morley College was established in 1889 to offer a varied range of adult education to the local community in Waterloo and North Southwark. Over the twentieth century, it has specialised in the liberal arts alongside basic education. The college is a charity with most of its funding provided by the Inner London Education Authority until 1990. Funding responsibility then passed to the London Residuary Body (LRB). The College has around 9,000 part-time students.

A new principal, Bev Walters, took up the post in 1991 as the third principal in four years. He arrived with a personal strategy of phased change. The LRB's deliberate strategy was to install a new principal, make the college less dependent on the public purse, and do all the major restructuring in one term.

The principal's response was not to confront the LRB and tell them that their agenda was unworkable. What he did was to secure more space through the inevitably time-consuming appointment of new heads of department. As the new heads of department arrived, they were asked to draw together development plans building on the college's existing ethos. The ethos acted as a touchstone and prevented the proliferation of other, unrelated strategies. The heads of department were also able to bring in opportunities for more vocationally oriented and qualification-based work. At the same time, anomalies such as orchestras not paying for their practice facilities were cleared up, showing a commitment to financial control.

The principal's strategy was both emergent and deliberate. He deliberately created space and allowed the ideas of the heads of department to emerge in that space. He was able to satisfy the funder and, just as importantly, to bring in new work and widen the base of the college. The presence in the background of the LRB and its deliberate funding and organisational strategy helped as a catalyst for change. A joint college governors/LRB executive committee monitored progress.

Emergent strategy allows the organisation to learn new strengths and to take opportunities. Deliberate strategy allows the organisation to review the pattern, perspective or position that has emerged and to decide how to take it forward. In a creative and flexible organisational climate, deliberate and emergent strategies can interact to produce 'umbrella strategies'. Coupling learning and control in this way is a great source of strength for organisations who are able to pursue both kinds of strategy.

Exercise 2   Assessing deliberate and emergent strategy

1 Read your organisation's strategy documents. If your organisation does not have an explicit strategy, look instead at its policy statements.

2 Think about your organisation's emergent strategy. Over the past two or three years, are there two or three patterns that have emerged?

3 Compare the deliberate and emergent strategies. Has your organisation done what it said it would or would not do? Have there been unintended consequences? Do the actions which have been taken fit with the organisation's values? What has your organisation learnt from its emergent strategy?

4 Ask someone else in your organisation for their views on the deliberate and emergent strategies you have identified. This is important to give you another perspective to compare with your own.

5 Keep the results of this exercise to compare with later exercises in the book and to help explain the strategy process to other staff in your organisation.

The benefits of planning

The planning dimension of strategy has a number of clear benefits. The organisation as a whole is examined. Inevitably people's day to day concerns are with their own areas of responsibility. Strategic planning acts like a helicopter which allows people to view the organisation as a complete entity and as others see it – achievements and blemishes alike.

Daily pressures frequently force people to restrict themselves to what is going on inside the organisation. As a consequence they may miss real threats or tremendous opportunities in the outside world. Planning can enable some people to gain greater security from new sources and from external changes. They are then better placed to develop the flexibility and capability in the organisation to change direction if necessary.

Planning can lend a new perspective to the organisation's crises and trouble spots. It can lead to an assessment of priorities and a review of how resources are targeted. For those involved in the process, it can involve second order learning. This means that the focus is not just on solving individual problems as they arise but on learning how to tackle problems systematically by spotting patterns of behaviour and so identifying the underlying causes.

Examples – the benefits of planning

Abbeyfield Society

An example of a strategic plan produced principally for internal reasons is that of the Abbeyfield Society. The Abbeyfield movement exists to provide those who are elderly and alone with homes within the companionship of small households. One main objective of the strategy exercise was to develop a senior management team. The planning process was initially confined to staff and then a draft set of proposals was presented to the wider Abbeyfield movement. The plan has resulted in five departments being created including a new one responsible for information and public affairs.

Civic Trust

The Civic Trust was established in 1957 as a response to what it saw as insensitive urban development. It has a mission to care for the places that form the backdrop to everyday life and sees one of its strengths as its ability to look ahead. In 1966, it foresaw that areas as well as buildings of character needed special care. The outcome was the creation of conservation areas, of which there are now more than 8,000 in the UK.

The changing nature of planning

The words 'strategy' and 'planning' used automatically to be put together, rather like Morecambe and Wise! Traditional strategy was something that could be planned to the nth degree. Current trends could be confidently predicted. Forecasts could be made to three decimal places. But things have changed. This rather inflexible and unresponsive long-range planning is now seen as something to be avoided. Taking the current view to an extreme, it has been argued that strategy is by definition something you cannot plan.

How has this shift in thinking come about? In the more stable past, many organisations, even voluntary organisations, were able to decide their objectives and then allocate the resources needed to achieve them, safe in the assumption that the world was changing only slowly.

The traditional approach to planning has been undermined by accelerating change that is beyond the control of organisations. Charles Handy describes joining Shell as a management trainee. He was told that if he did well he could expect to run a particular overseas subsidiary. By the time he left Shell, the job did not exist, the subsidiary did not exist, and the country did not exist. Volatility to this degree is being felt by many voluntary organisations.

Example – the changing environment

RNIB

The Royal National Institute for the Blind (RNIB) was established in 1868. The growth in its activities has been steady but gradual, starting with the introduction of Braille, a raised type for the blind. In 1918 it opened its first school followed by other schools and a commercial college. In 1962 the RNIB started its eye donor scheme.

The organisation's growth was fuelled by a steady flow of legacies. These legacies, plus the fact that the number of visually impaired people is usually fairly constant, provided a stable background against which to plan. However, the circumstances are now less stable. The average age of blind people, and therefore the likely degree of other disabilities, is increasing. In addition other organisations have set up in the same field and compete both to attract funds and to provide services.

It is the current rate of change that makes people believe that strategy cannot be planned. Events will render the plan out of date before the ink is dry. Nevertheless, we believe that all organisations can and should plan because what can be planned has only changed, not disappeared completely.

Traditional planning set the ends first and then tried to find the means that would achieve those ends. In a volatile environment, the reverse may be true. Think about the following story. You are on a journey. You have your end, which is your destination. You have a means of transport, such as your car, to get you there. As long as your physical environment is predictable, the journey can be planned. But suppose that you find yourself in a barren and inhospitable land. Your car has to be abandoned. Your purpose suddenly changes, and becomes to find your way out of that land. You choose whatever in the car will be most useful for that. A good map, even if you have remembered to bring one, may not be enough. You may have to make choices because there is a limit to what you can carry. Suddenly the means have become much more important. The end is no longer a fixed point. Anywhere outside the wilderness will do.

In a volatile environment, planning provides a sharper focus and purpose for an organisation. Planning is about options. In an uncertain world, organisations need to be quick to learn, flexible and responsive. There is much less time for front-line staff to consult management about what to do.

So development of the organisation's people, staff and volunteers, becomes critical. The skills they need in a world of rapid change are very different from those demanded by a slower world. Judgement, for example, has a clearer place within the overall framework of strategic planning. Volatility often produces a need for shared values, mutual trust and a strong sense of direction. Abraham Lincoln was once accused of stumbling along. He retorted that this might be true but 'we are stumbling in the right direction'.

Action points

Below are five statements about strategy. Without looking back at what you have just read, tick those that you think are true:

1 Organisations are likely to learn more when their strategy is deliberate.
2 Organisations are likely to learn more when their strategy is emergent.
3 Strategy is mainly about budgeting.
4 Strategy is a fancy word for planning.
5 Strategy is about what you do with your organisation's resources.

Now look back at the definitions given in this chapter and see whether you want to alter any of your answers.

Our own answers are:
- For 1 and 2, it depends on your organisation which is true. In general, learning is greatest from the interaction of both forms of strategy.
- For 3, 4 and 5, none of these definitions is adequate. Strategy is much more than that.

Chapter 2
The Process of Strategy

Planning is everything, the plan is nothing.

Eisenhower

This chapter describes why planning, the *process* of developing strategy, is valuable. It explains why it is important to involve as many people as possible in planning and then deals with the objections that may be raised. A description of the process is followed by consideration of who takes responsibility for planning. This leads on to how to plan and the various rules it is vital to follow. The starting point of the process is 'planning to plan', followed by 'when', the timetable for planning.

Why plan?

Changes in strategy require involvement

Chapter 1 described how the increasing volatility of the environment has changed the nature of strategy. In an uncertain world, what matters is that members of organisations, and hence the organisations themselves, learn quickly and are flexible and responsive.

This applies especially to staff who are not managers. Previously, if there was a problem it was referred up and down through the hierarchy. Now there is often less time available for staff to consult managers. So the people on the ground need to be given the confidence and skills to handle problems themselves. The skills they need in a world of rapid change are very different from those which used to be required. Intuition, for example, becomes more important. There need to be shared values, a strong sense of purpose, and mutual trust.

The lesson is that people from all levels of the organisation should be involved in planning strategy. Top-down planning, where the strategy is handed down from on high by senior management, does not work in a fast moving world. Senior managers provide the perspective of the organisation as a whole, but they cannot possess all the information they need to plan properly. As a result, any such plan is usually a 'wish list', untempered by practicality. Those involved in an operation day after day are often best placed to say what changes are possible, and how best to make them.

The second reason for involving a wide range of people in the process is that they will be needed to carry out the strategy. How well they carry it out will depend on how committed they feel, how far they feel it is their strategy.

In a large organisation, involving everyone directly in setting strategy is impossible. Proposals for dealing with this will be found in the section on the planning team below, and in Chapter 6.

A small organisation will not have many levels, but it will have an even greater need to muster all the potential energy and commitment. This means involving as many groups as possible, such as users, trustees and volunteers.

Important as involvement is, there may be circumstances when it is difficult to continue it through all the stages of decision making. An example might be where part of the organisation is at risk. Only an exceptionally open and supportive culture would be able to involve people in discussing the fate of their own jobs. However, if involvement can be maintained, it should improve the quality of the decision.

The benefits of the planning process

If the recommendations of this book are followed, you will be bringing people together with sufficient time, without interruptions, and with an open agenda. This paves the way for two benefits.

Fixed ideas are challenged

We all tend to have relatively fixed views about the world. Planning helps to challenge preconceptions by forcing people to pay attention to different assumptions and possibilities. For instance, look at Figure 1. If you have not seen it before, you are likely to see either two people, or a vase. Once you have seen one, this sticks in your mind and it becomes hard to see the other.

Figure I Rubin's Example of Visual Reversal

Example – changing preconceptions

Shell

In 1984 Shell persuaded their managers to think about what the world would be like if the price of oil was $15 a barrel. This was difficult, since the actual price was $28 and the managers were convinced it would stay there. But the exercise became invaluable in 1986, when the price of a barrel of oil fell to $10. Shell's response was faster and better than that of other oil companies because they had already thought through the possibilities.

We also tend to have fixed ideas about solutions. For example, some people look first at the organisation's structure; others always concentrate on the culture. Thinking about the problem in a different way may inspire unusual solutions.

Teams are built and strengthened

Planning with involvement, as we recommend, means that people who do not normally work together find themselves doing so. They learn about other parts of the organisation. Planning will involve them in looking at the organisation and its universe, often for the first time, and in trying to agree on a common view with the other participants in the team.

Why not plan?

The circumstances in which planning is likely to fail are few in number, although they occur quite frequently. In each case there should be some possibility of changing the circumstances so that planning can succeed. This section lists these circumstances and covers the many objections to planning that may be raised in your organisation.

Planning is likely to fail when:

- trustees, the board of trustees and top management do not believe in it;
- top management takes all the decisions, so that there is no tradition of involvement;

- survival is under immediate threat and the organisation needs everyone to concentrate on the present;
- top management is irreconcilably split over fundamental issues.

Objections

First, here are some substantial objections, with our replies.

We are too busy worrying about today to have time to think about tomorrow
If you do not think at all about tomorrow, there are two likely outcomes. You may not be around tomorrow, because your approach will increase the number and severity of your crises until your organisation is unable to cope. Even if you do survive, you will lose your sense of direction. There are several examples later in this book of organisations distracted from their original mission by crises or by opportunism. Opportunism is a way of living day by day. It has a place, but only when accompanied by a strong sense of purpose, reinforced by if not created by planning.

Strategic planning is rational: the real world is not
To use a medical analogy, strategic planning is both diagnosis and cure. It provides an X-ray of the organisation, its capacity to prosper and its motivations. If the diagnosis is correct it can contribute to a cure. In medicine, a successful cure will depend on intangibles like the patient's state of mind as much as on rational factors. In the voluntary sector in particular, planning has to be based on the values of the organisation. It can then provide a framework for understanding and managing the non-rational aspects of the organisation.

For the voluntary sector, strategic planning is an alien private sector import
The question should not be 'where does it come from?', but 'is it useful?' As we discussed in the Introduction, strategy began as a military concept. It was taken over by the private sector which adapted its concepts and language. The public sector has generally

been able to use it as an essential tool in preserving public sector values and likewise, the voluntary sector can take over and adapt the private sector approach. This would not be possible if planning was indeed alien to the voluntary sector.

Strategic planning helps you to grow – we're shrinking
Strategic planning has advantages whatever your situation. If you are shrinking, strategic planning can help you to take opportunities to manage the contraction, stabilise and then grow again if appropriate.

Other objections

Here are some typical objections that might be put forward by staff, volunteers, or the board of trustees:

- This is just paper. It has nothing to do with action.
- This is too academic. It is all for people with educational qualifications.
- It is just an excuse for getting consultants in.
- We have managed perfectly well for 15 years without a strategic plan.
- We all know where we are going. We don't need to write it down in some fat document.
- The last chief executive spent all her time on this and look what happened to her.
- Strategies are a straitjacket.
- Strategies are for senior management, not me.
- It's just a wish list we cannot afford to do.

Using objections

Objections have value in two ways. They test your understanding of what strategic planning is all about. (What you have read so far should enable you to answer all the objections above except perhaps the one about consultants, a subject which will be covered later in this chapter.) Objections from those that speak out are also invaluable in working out how to sell the idea to the organisation at large. It is important to check two points. Is the stated objection the true objection, or does another concern underlie it? Is the objection typical of those likely to come from the organisation as a whole or not; for example, it may represent the views of middle managers, the only ones who feel able to speak out.

What is planning?

Figure 2 The Stages of Planning

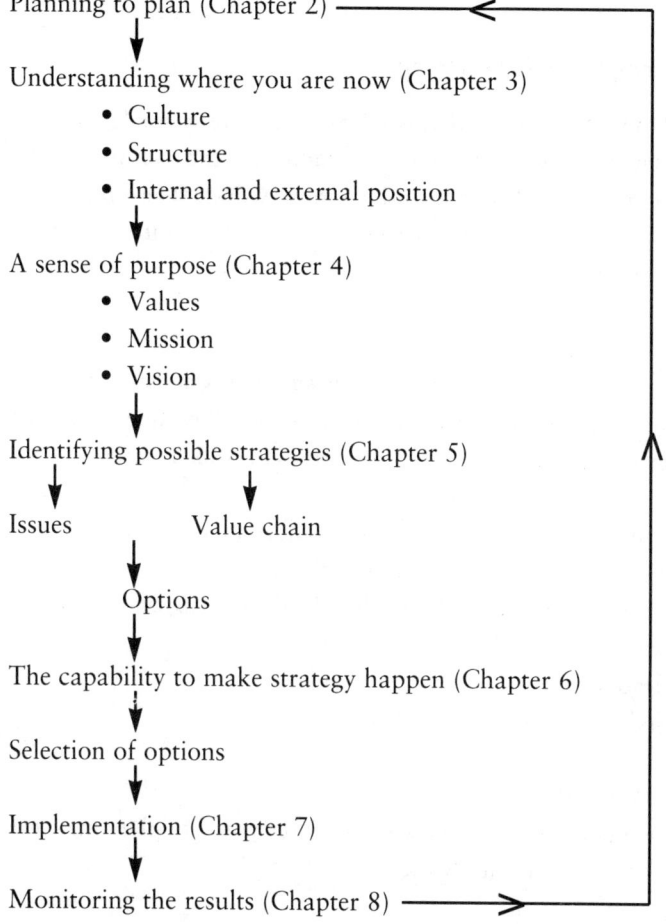

Planning to plan (Chapter 2)

Understanding where you are now (Chapter 3)
- Culture
- Structure
- Internal and external position

A sense of purpose (Chapter 4)
- Values
- Mission
- Vision

Identifying possible strategies (Chapter 5)

Issues   Value chain

Options

The capability to make strategy happen (Chapter 6)

Selection of options

Implementation (Chapter 7)

Monitoring the results (Chapter 8)

Figure 2 illustrates the stages in the planning process. Each stage is described in detail in the relevant chapter. As we have already said, this is an iterative sequence. Later stages influence earlier stages, as well as the other way around. Some of an organisation's values, for example, may only emerge when contentious issues are debated. So each stage needs to be reviewed for its impact on previous stages. The process as a whole is also iterative. When you have been through all the stages, you should review the entire process and use your experience to improve it the next time around. This aspect is covered in more detail in Chapter 8.

Different emphases for planning

So far planning has been discussed as if it were a single, uniform process. In fact, it will vary according to the nature of the organisation and the demands of the outside world. The next section illustrates some possible emphases for both the strategy and the process by which it is put together.

Survival

If the organisation is in decline, or if its survival is at stake, the need is for a simple plan that concentrates on the small number of factors that are critical to survival. A turnround plan is likely to include:

- restructuring for greater control and reduced costs;
- measures of critical short-term objectives;
- simple, clear messages about the depth of the crisis and the solution;
- active leadership;
- improved promotion and marketing.

Imposed planning

If an outside body is able to pressure or force you into planning, your first requirement is to satisfy them.

Example – imposed planning

In 1988 the Arts Council introduced an incentive funding scheme. The prerequisite for application was a three-year plan, with the funding as an incentive. This was mostly very successful, but arts organisations inevitably had to fit in with Arts Council requirements:

> The work for which we were offered an award is carried out through a subsidiary, profit-making company which covenants the whole of its profits back to the charitable arts company and our community work. The fact that the incentive funding scheme looks at the gross income of the subsidiary company rather than its net profits means that we are inclined to take on more work even though the profit margins on some of the work are not so good.
>
> *(Incentive Funding,* The Arts Council, 1990)

Dealing with conflict

If there is a great deal of conflict within the organisation, use methods that build consensus or secure a clear majority (see Chapters 6 and 7).

Dealing with uncertainty

Your strategy may depend on whether or not you can retain a large sum in grant aid. You might then find it useful to create scenarios or pictures of possible futures to help you to think through how you would behave with and without the money (see Chapter 5).

Stakeholders

Your stakeholders are the people or other organisations that have an interest or a 'stake' in your organisation. They may be inside the organisation – volunteers, staff, trustees, subscribers and so on. Or they may be outside, such as clients and funders.

The value of a formal exercise to list your stakeholders is that you may identify some that you had not previously considered. This may be because 'out of sight is out of mind'. The Department for Education, for instance, reminds schools to consider prospective parents as well as current parents. Alternatively, it may be that a particular stakeholder is not noticed because they are too obvious. Until recently, for instance, the Royal National Lifeboat Institution had never thought to ask the people they rescued for views on the service.

All stakeholders have some influence over the organisation. The more they are in a position to express their concerns, the greater their influence. Very powerful stakeholders, such as a substantial funder, will often try to have a large say in the organisation's strategy. The merger of three separate projects to create the London Advice Service Alliance (LASA) is a case in point. Although the merger had both supporters and opponents, it was the main funder which carried the day. One of the most important tasks of a voluntary organisation is to balance the often competing interests of stakeholders.

The easiest way to find out what your stakeholders think of you is to ask them. The British Red Cross did a survey to find out what its image was with the public, a stakeholder. The result can be summarised as 'best known – least understood'. Traidcraft plc is an alternative trading organisation which imports and distributes handicrafts, stationery and other products from the 'third world'. It has recently carried out a social audit that involved asking all its major stakeholders what they thought that Traidcraft's objectives should be, and how well it was meeting them. Traidcraft learnt, for instance, that 'third world' producer groups rated communication as very important, and that some groups in the Philippines felt communication was impeded because their output was consolidated for shipment by another Filipino group, which was Traidcraft's main point of contact.

However, you may find that some stakeholders, even when you have identified them, may not be in a position to express their concerns. Sir Len Peach, when chief executive of the Health Service, suggested that, 'it may be argued that the whole of society constitutes our shareholding body.' Society may be able to express its concerns through its political representatives. What about future generations, with whom some environmental groups are deeply concerned?

Exercise 3 Identifying the stakeholders of the Vehicle Inspectorate

Cover up the next paragraph. Consider the Vehicle Inspectorate (one of the government's Executive Agencies, responsible for vehicle testing and roadworthiness enforcement). Make a list of its stakeholders.

Answer
Parliament; ministers; Department of Transport; operators of heavy goods and public service vehicles; owners of MOT testing garages; trade associations; and staff.

Exercise 4 Identifying your stakeholders

1 List your main stakeholders.
2 Position each on the diagram below according to how you see their influence and importance. Note that importance and influence are very different. For example, the trustees may be very important, but exert little influence.

```
High  │
      │
Importance │
      │
Low   │
      └─────────────────────────
      Low                   High
              Influence
```

3   For each stakeholder:

- List the criteria by which they evaluate your organisation. State your own view, and if possible ask the stakeholder.
- Say how well you are satisfying each criterion (well, average, or badly).

Managing your stakeholders

If there are important or influential stakeholders whose criteria you are not satisfying well, this knowledge will be useful when you are identifying possible strategies (see Chapter 5). How do you handle this problem?

It is the prerogative of voluntary organisations to decide which people they exist to help. They should not, however, ignore other stakeholders who have power. If a powerful group is not satisfied, they may stop the organisation serving the stakeholders it most wants to help.

Example – ignoring stakeholders

The professionals of the fisheries and wildlife department of a US state thought that their chief stakeholders were the fish and the deer. As a result, stakeholders such as anglers and hunters felt ignored. They retaliated by trying to have the department's powers and resources reduced.

The more disparate the criteria by which different stakeholders judge you, the more you are likely to be pulled in different directions. The best tactic is twofold. First, link your stakeholders with the organisation. This is why, for example, the National Federation of Women's Institutes is encouraging key regional members to visit its headquarters in London. Secondly, bring your stakeholders together. These actions will encourage the aims of different stakeholders to converge, both with those of the organisation and with each other.

Examples – links with stakeholders

Brooke Hospital for Animals
The Brooke Hospital for Animals organises tours so that its supporters can visit its overseas centres. These strengthen the

relations between several stakeholders: supporters, staff, animals, and their owners. Supporters who have seen where and how the money raised has been spent tend to be the most committed. Another link the organisation encourages is between supporters and trustees, through an annual tea party at the House of Commons.

Tioxide

Another example of this is the grants made by the Tioxide chemicals group on Teesside to local schools. The activities funded included shared reading schemes, mother and toddler groups, the development of wildlife areas, craft skills demonstrations, 'pie and pea' suppers for senior citizens, and healthy eating cookbooks. All were designed to link the schools with their stakeholders.

The role of the planner

The role of the planner is to help others to plan. Paradoxically, the role of a planner is not to plan. Planners and consultants tend to be articulate and numerate. They face a strong temptation to believe that they can write a better plan than front-line management and staff. But the organisation will never be committed to the plan unless people on the ground feel that it is theirs, because they prepared it.

The planner's role involves the following tasks:

- Establishing credibility, for example by using knowledge of the subject to help the organisation's staff to tackle their own issues, or by ensuring good communication with all departments.
- Explaining the importance of strategic planning.
- Making the process clear. It may take people unused to planning some time to become familiar with it. Managers especially tend to concentrate on content and not on process. Pressure for results often leads to a lack of time or inclination to allow the reflection that planning requires. People may need to see that support is coming from the top before they can take it seriously.

- Encouraging people to find out about planning for themselves, for example by looking through this book.
- Acting as a catalyst, as devil's advocate, as the 'licensed revolutionary' who 'speaks the unspeakable'.
- Ensuring that problems are correctly identified and defined – they may not be what they first seem.
- Opening up a wider range of options. Managers tend to think in terms of solutions rather than alternatives.
- Making sure that others plan, by ensuring that someone takes responsibility for each task and that these responsibilities are fulfilled.

Who the planner should be

The description of the planner's role is a guide to the sort of person required. He or she needs to be both capable of being objective and seen as being so. Any suspicion of a hidden agenda would undermine effectiveness.

The planning team

Planning is likely to be improved if the planner reports to a group other than the board of trustees. The planning team should fulfil the following requirements:

- It should be representative, both of parts of the organisation (so you may want to include members of the board of trustees) and of levels within the organisation. Consider whether to involve outside stakeholders, especially users.
- It should be capable of drawing on ideas and experience from across the organisation.
- It should ideally include some people with experience of other organisations.
- Members should be generally open to new ideas.
- It should be seen as an opportunity for staff development.

- It should include people able to perform the various roles that teams require. All the roles are explained in detail in Meredith Belbin's excellent book, *Management Teams: Why They Succeed or Fail*, but they can be simplified into four:
  1 the Captain, whose main role is to encourage
  2 the Expert, the source of ideas and analysis
  3 the Administrator, who keeps the team organised
  4 the Driver, who pushes the task through

Example – team roles

The Business Network
The management group of the Business Network, a network for those interested in a holistic view of business, did an exercise to establish what roles its members played. They were startled to find that they were all Experts, and that only the hard-pressed secretary was making sure that things actually got done.

The team will need to have status and easy access to top management. In forming the team, remember that anti-discriminatory practice is as important here as elsewhere in voluntary organisations. The best size for the group is likely to be between six and ten people. The frequency of meetings obviously depends on the pace of progress, but is unlikely to be less often than once every six weeks.

Other teams or working groups may be required later on. These may be to tackle particular issues (see Chapter 5) or aspects of implementation (see Chapter 7).

How to plan

The process of planning is not easy. In one survey of companies, 87 per cent reported that they felt frustrated with their planning systems. In another, 25 per cent said that their planning staff had had a negative effect on their strategic decisions.

This kind of frustration can be avoided by following these seven rules.

1 Lead from the top

Planning must be authorised and encouraged from the very top of the organisation. There are three aspects to this: legitimacy, justification and energy.

- Legitimacy is created by the director and/or board of trustees stating firmly that this is something they want the organisation to do. They also need to legitimise the planner and the planning team, who may as a result of taking on these roles have to give up some of what they were previously doing.
- Justification is created when the benefits of planning are spelt out clearly.
- Energy is created when top managers are also seen to be doing something about the planning process. It is especially valuable to have a champion, a senior person who pushes and pulls a planning process into being. (Should the champion leave the organisation during the planning cycle, top management needs to be aware of the likely loss of impetus.) Planning must not only be wanted, it must be seen to be wanted. The director must be seen to be submitting to the same discipline as everyone else. Managers tend to wait and see how seriously the director is taking planning before they decide how much effort they will put into it.

2 Ensure ownership

As we said at the start of this chapter, the plan needs to be owned by the members of the organisation if they are to care about implementing it successfully. The more open and involving the process is, the greater the ownership. Involvement follows a sequence:

- informing people
- listening to their views
- formal consultation – eg through an attitude survey
- asking them to be part of the process
- asking them to help run the process
- asking them to help design the process
- letting them run the process
- letting them design the process

Exercise 5 Measuring involvement

1 Where has your organisation reached in the involvement sequence?
2 What is your evidence for this?
3 How far would your organisation like to go in this sequence?
4 What is your evidence for this?
5 If there is a gap between your current position and where you would like to be, how could it be bridged?

Note that we are not saying that every organisation should aim to reach the end of the sequence. This may not be feasible; even if it is, it will involve lots of people and slow the process down. Each organisation will decide how far it wants to take involvement, depending on its style.

3 Manage conflict

The principle of openness means that conflict must be brought out into the open, not suppressed. Techniques for managing conflict are described in Chapters 6 and 7.

Keep outsiders (funders, users, etc) informed throughout the process. Their concerns will be far harder to deal with if they are not voiced until the end of the process.

4 Provide resources

Most voluntary organisations will not have specific planning staff. On the other hand, a good plan is not produced by someone sparing half a day a week from a busy schedule. There needs to be someone who makes sure that planning takes place. The person undertaking the planning needs to be able to give enough time to this. (Although this person is referred to as the 'planner', this is not to suggest that this is a full-time role or job title.)

5 Relate planning to other activities

Planning should not be led by budgeting. If it is, plans tend to get produced by extrapolating next year's numbers and to stress numbers rather than quality of thinking. The financial aspects of planning are covered in Chapter 7. Nevertheless, planning does need to be integrated with the organisation's other processes: structure, reward systems, and so on.

6 Don't go overboard

We have put forward many reasons why all voluntary organisations should do some strategic planning. However, it is not a cure for all ills. It is possible to take it too far. One danger is too much planning, leading to strategy fatigue. New approaches need time to work. Plants pulled up too often to see how they are growing cannot grow. If the planning handle is cranked too often, the process becomes too mechanical and the organisation loses its sensitivity to real change. Another danger is having too grand and glossy a plan. This can inhibit flexibility and make the task of implementation look impossibly forbidding.

7 Avoid rigidity

Another danger lies in the mere fact that having a strategy and making it explicit create resistance to change. 'The plan says X, so we can't do Y until we redo the plan next year.' Make sure you retain flexibility.

Planning to plan

Skills

Successful planning involves using a wide range of skills. Some of these are listed in Table 1.

Table I Planning Skills

Personal	Facilitating
	Negotiating
	Surfacing conflict
	Resolving conflict
	Influencing
	Working in a team
	Training
Presentational	Summarising
	Designing graphics
	Making presentations
	Interacting with a group
Analytic	Research
	Data collection
	Synthesising information
Systemic	Using IT (information technology)
	Budgeting

Exercise 6 Identifying skills

Many of us are modest in our assessment of the skills we possess, and do not realise the extent of the skills we acquire and use in everyday life.

Think back over the last fortnight. What is the most

complicated activity you had to do? List the separate tasks that the activity involved. Against each task list the skills it took to carry out that task.

Here is an example to give you the idea. A participant in a training course that we ran had her car stolen. Coping with the problem required several skills, including:

- *personal organisation* – arranging to collect the car once the police had found it;
- *logistics* – having the car towed to a near-by garage;
- *persuasion* – to get her brother to do the shopping;
- *talking in other people's language* – to the police and insurers.

You may not have all the skills that you need yourself. This does not matter, provided that you can find what you need among the people who are prepared to be involved. Below we consider possible sources for resources of all kinds, and then discuss the possibility of bringing in a consultant if there is skill and knowledge that you cannot find elsewhere.

Other resources

Planning differs from day to day activities in both the resources you need and the range of places where you can seek them. You are unlikely to feel able to ring a trustee or trustee board member and ask them to help you to fill in an accounts book. But you can ring them and ask whether they will attend or facilitate a planning day.

Table 2 contains a list of sources and resources, not designed to be complete, just to stimulate you in your search.

Table 2 Sources and Resources

Volunteers – they may have specialist knowledge that you do not know about.

Secondees – contact REACH (the Retired Executives Action Clearing House).

Equipment – whiteboards, overhead projectors, etc.

Photocopying – don't ask the authors where the drafts of this book were photocopied!

Information and advice – see the note on the services provided by NCVO on page ii. As an example of how far afield it may be worth looking, the UK-based Polden Puckham Charitable Foundation joined the US Environmental Grantmakers Association, for advice no British body could provide.

Courses – eg those run by NCVO and the Directory of Social Change.

Sponsorship – eg the Association for Business Sponsorship of the Arts (ABSA).

Any organisation, similar to your organisation in some way and with which you are content to share your experience, which has also undertaken planning. NCVO will put you in touch with such an organisation if it knows of one.

Peers in other organisations.

Computer software.

Consultants (see below for how to use them).

Other books – including those mentioned in the introduction and Appendix 4 – and journals, such as *Long Range Planning*, the journal of the Strategic Planning Society.

Stages of planning to plan

- Decide what emphasis the plan is likely to have. This in turn will decide your time horizon. If the organisation is in crisis, the plan may only be for a year or two. If you have a well defined vision, your plan could cover ten years or more.
- Introduce the idea and the benefits to your people, especially in relation to areas where the need for change is already apparent. Use the results of exercise 1 on page 4.
- Evaluate what the plan would mean for the organisation (the extra work involved, other resources required, etc).
- Develop a commitment (see Chapter 6).

- Reach an agreement. This should be on paper, and should:
  - commit key decision-makers to giving enough time to the process of planning; to ensure that this is quality time, we strongly recommend that these people spend at least a day together, away from the office;
  - set out a timetable covering the various stages, including meetings and reports;
  - lay out the format for at least the first day of the process;
  - ensure that there are sufficient resources available;
  - say who will do what, and in what order.

Workshops

Well planned strategy workshops can simplify the process and reduce the time that it takes. All the stages up to implementation could be combined into three one-day workshops. The first two could be undertaken over a weekend, although ideally there should be time for research and reflection between them. The workshops are decribed in Table 3.

Table 3 Strategy Workshops

Strategy starter workshop, covering:
- understanding where you are now
- values
- mission
- vision
- action to be taken

Strategy development workshop, covering:
- identifying issues
- strategic options for dealing with each issue
- choice of strategies
- framework for the strategic plan
- action to be taken

Workshop on plans, covering
- review of the draft strategic plan
- initial development of action plans for implementation
- action to be taken

Points to note in planning and running workshops
- All workshops will be more effective if held away from the office.
- If you use a facilitator, choose the person for his or her skills and not status.
- Secure agreement at the start of each workshop on appropriate confidentiality.
- Start each workshop with a warm-up routine – an icebreaker, a game, or a puzzle.
- Be aware that top managers may find it uncomfortable to have difficult issues aired so publicly. Encourage them to keep an open mind.
- Others may be constrained by the presence of top managers and will need encouragement to open up.
- Work in small groups wherever possible.
- Have frequent breaks. This not only takes account of our short attention span, it also enables informal communication to supplement communication within the sessions.
- Build in evaluation of each workshop. Ask people for their views both at the end of the workshop and a fortnight later.

Using a consultant

Consultants have two main attributes: process skills and technical knowledge. These attributes are very different in nature, and consultants tend to be stronger on one than the other. Be clear about which you want. Process skills are skills in understanding, and in helping the organisation to understand, interpersonal relationships and their effect on the strategic process. Technical knowledge is likely to be knowledge of particular strategies, such as how to increase your membership. It follows that consultants who offer this are likely to be required at a later stage, when strategies have been selected, than consultants offering to help you with the process of making strategy.

Consultants also possess the neutrality that comes with being an outsider. An insider may experience difficulties, especially if there are differing and strongly held views on where an organisation should go. The Youth Hostel Association (YHA), for example, used a consultant in the early 1980s. It feels that his value lay far more in stimulating change, because he was listened to as an outsider, than in his actual proposals. Note that a consultant who is involved with an organisation for some time, especially with a single point of contact within the organisation, may cease to be seen as neutral. Consultants are not the only type of outsider that can perform this role. For the YHA, its external solicitors acted as unbiased advisers in relation to its response to the 1992 Charities Act.

A second benefit of an outsider is that a consultant may be able to pick up and make sense of themes and patterns, for example in attitudes, that have been missed by insiders.

There are dangers in using consultants. You should not usually ask a consultant to write your plan for you. You may be given a plan 'off the shelf', full of standard recommendations. The result would also be a lack of 'ownership' by the organisation, making it very unlikely that the plan would be carried out successfully. Only if these factors do not matter would it be right to use a consultant for this purpose. An example of such a circumstance might be if a funder requires you to produce a plan at short notice as an alternative to having funding discontinued. Such circumstances are extremely rare.

More generally, the more the consultants deal with content, and the less with process, the greater the danger that they take over too much of the planning. In one organisation it became impossible to raise key issues because the response was always, 'We can't touch that – the consultants are looking at it.'

Finally, a cautionary tale. The London Advice Service Alliance (LASA) is very non-hierarchical. So when it briefed a consultant to advise the organisation on structure, it said that having a director was out of the question. The consultant refused to be circumscribed and duly recommended a director. LASA now has a director, and feels that it was in fact the right course to take.

Recruiting a consultant

NCVO holds a list of consultants to which you can refer. Some guidelines are:

- Do not be overimpressed by flashy clothes and a sharp presentation.
- Produce a written specification of what you want the consultant to do.
- Estimate how long the job will take and how much you are prepared to pay for it.
- Understand the consultant's values and how he or she would handle a clash with your organisation's values.
- How do they work – do they have favourite tools or strategies?
- What responsibility will they take for achieving results?
- Establish their experience in the areas that interest you.
- Take up references.

Action points

- Decide whether strategic planning is an event for trustees, staff/volunteers on their own, or both groups.
- Top management should choose a planner and a planning team.

For the planner:
- Decide what objections you may face and how to meet them.
- Decide whether the emphasis of your planning is clear yet.
- Identify your stakeholders and their expectations of you.
- Identify the resources you have available.
- Decide whether to use a consultant.
- Reach an agreement to plan.

Chapter 3
Understanding Where You are Now

We must ask where we are and whither we are tending.

Abraham Lincoln

This chapter will help you understand and analyse the present position of your organisation. Managing a voluntary organisation has been compared to driving on a motorway. It is easy to get trapped in the fast lane. It is necessary to come off the motorway and refuel. It is necessary to find time for thinking and assessing where your organisation is.

The chapter is in two parts. The first concentrates on the significant influence which culture and structure have on strategy. The second part provides a range of strategic planning tools and techniques, and explains their value and how to use them.

Culture

Organisational culture can be simply defined as 'the way we do things around here'. It includes the organisation's style and feel, shared values, routines, myths and symbols. It can inhibit or subvert actions that run against it. Cultures are not static. They emerge, grow, mature, alter and die.

If the strategy tries to change 'the way we do things around here', there is likely to be fierce resistance. So the customs and traditions that are blocking strategic change need to be identified. The difficulty is that culture is a central part of the deeper character of all organisations. As it tends to lie just below the surface, the precise culture can be difficult to convey accurately to those unfamiliar with the organisation. It is difficult to overstate the impact of organisational culture on strategic planning.

An existing strategy can be a deeply entrenched perspective in the organisation. To become effective, the strategy may need to influence the way the organisation considers and weighs opinions and changes in its environment and itself. In short, such a strategy will seek major cultural change.

Example – underlying culture

The story goes that a new chief executive found a foreman shaking a worker by the throat and yelling, 'If you make just one more mistake, you're out, I'll kick you into the street.' The foreman was hastily sent on an interpersonal skills course as part of the human resource strategy. Three months later, the chief executive found the foreman shaking another worker by the throat and yelling, 'If you make just one more mistake, you rat, I'll kick you into the street. By the way, how's your mother-in-law's cold?'

The skills that the foreman was taught simply formed a veneer over his behaviour. They did not change the underlying culture of the organisation which, in practice, had moulded his attitudes. Hence they were no more than skin deep.

Four types of culture

There are significant differences in organisational cultures. Charles Handy developed a framework for analysing culture which encompasses four common types of culture, all present in the voluntary sector: power culture, role culture, task culture and person culture.

Power culture

The power culture is often found in an organisation dominated by one person, in new organisations or those where the founder remains dominant. Power can be exercised benevolently in the mode of an extended family, or the style may be authoritarian and rest on rule by fear. The way Robert Maxwell ran his business was through a power culture.

Role culture

In a role culture, individual power is constrained by structure, hierarchy and procedure. The accent is on administration rather than leadership. The culture tends to be stable and bureaucratic and values consistency in the application of rules. It is efficient when the organisation's tasks and the outside world change little. Local government has a classic role culture. Where change is rapid, however, role cultures find it difficult to respond. People are too used to obeying the system to be good at changing the system itself.

Task culture

Power and role cultures tend to motivate people by rewarding or punishing them. Task cultures rely on people finding a much more powerful motivator in the quality of the work itself, or the context in which it is done. Focus on the task means a strong emphasis on problem solving and flexible teamwork to tackle the task of the moment. The task culture stresses people's ability to take the initiative and be creative. The risks of a task culture lie in unclear accountability and lack of direction. Organisations with matrix structures (referred to later in this chapter) seek to have a task culture, as do many aid and development organisations.

Person culture

The three cultures discussed so far are based on different ways of getting people to carry out their part of the purpose of the organisation. The person culture is so called because it puts the person and his or her purpose before that of the organisation. There tends to be a strong emphasis on values such as sharing and openness. Such trust and commitment usually depend on people having worked together for a long time. The disadvantage is that the emphasis on consensus means that conflict may be avoided even though it may be valuable in stimulating change. Person cultures can be found in some collective organisations in the voluntary sector.

Exercise 7   Diagnosing your organisation's culture

Fill in the chart below to indicate how the culture of your organisation is made up:

Type of culture	To what extent is the culture of your organisation of that type?	Examples of this type of culture in your organisation
	(H = high; M = medium; L = low)	
Power		
Role		
Task		
Person		

Social role

Another way of looking at organisations is in terms of their social role. Charles Handy has identified four main types of voluntary organisation – service delivery, campaigning, mutual support, and intermediary support. Strategic planning is relevant to each type of voluntary organisation but its value might lie in different areas:

- *Service delivery* – strategic planning is particularly relevant to contracting out, efficiency and control of services provided.

- *Campaigning* – strategic planning is important for planning within constraints and maintaining momentum. It ensures cohesion between individual campaigns. It keeps in place an overall sense of where the organisation is going.
- *Mutual support* – within this type of organisation, strategic planning is important for managing resources. It formalises *ad hoc* structures. It helps in shifting structure if organisations later evolve into campaigning or service delivery organisations.
- *Intermediary support* – strategic planning skills can be used to help others to make strategy and for the intermediary organisations themselves. It can promote good relations with other sectors of society, particularly funding bodies. It can define and secure a niche.

Evolution

Voluntary organisations do change their character over time. The age and ageing of voluntary organisations (not the people in them!) can affect strategy and its formulation.

Many organisations are set up to provide self-help to the founding members. A good number then evolve into a second stage of service delivery and/or campaigning organisation. The transition is almost always difficult. It is not easy, for instance, for those who have always worked hard to help themselves to accept that others should receive a service without having to work for it. Similarly when employing staff, trustees often have difficulty with the idea of paying staff for what they have previously done without payment.

Other events that mark a shift to another stage include taking on your first member of staff, changing premises, and winning long or significant contracts or grants.

Example – evolution

The National Association of Development Education Centres was established in the late 1970s. It took on its first staff member in the early 1980s while continuing to emphasise its role as a network. Extra staff were gained through a European Community funded project – 'Building from Strengths'. The organisation has now been merged with the development education sections of the relevant international non-governmental organisations to become the Development Education Association. This will be able to co-ordinate all development education.

Structure

Both the progress and the path of strategic planning will vary considerably depending on the type of structure the organisation has. Handy's classification of social roles implicitly stresses the importance of the service and campaigning divide among voluntary organisations. It is as important to look at the distinctions of structure. The particular structure is a good indicator of the likely complexity of the strategic planning process and goals.

Six types of structure

Voluntary organisations come in all shapes and sizes. Here we identify six types of voluntary organisation structure – simple, network, missionary, matrix, federal and role bureaucracy – and explain the usefulness of strategic planning for the different types of structure.

Simple

A simple organisation is a single unit dominated by one person, with little formalisation or standardisation. It is often a young organisation and usually small. For strategic planning, the key issues may well be whether the dominant individual(s) will accept the process. The culture is likely to be one of power.

Network or adhocracy

The environment of a network organisation is both complex and dynamic, with scope for managers and staff to be entrepreneurial and to take risks. To sustain itself, the organisation has to be able to innovate in complex ways. This means pulling together teams of people with different expertise. The expertise is so important that there is relatively little power at the top. Co-ordination is mainly through informal communication between experts. Given the diffuse nature of the organisation, strategic change that involves building alliances may be difficult. Networks will often find it difficult to hold a coherent view of the world. Network organisations tend to have a task culture.

Missionary

Missionary organisations are driven by their values and the desire to convert others to their views, and are not necessarily religious. Once new members acquire the values of the organisation, they are given freedom to make decisions. There is unlikely to be much specialisation. The organisation is likely to flourish in stable conditions and is unlikely to be young. Strategy will tend to be deliberate. Such organisations can exhibit aspects of the power culture.

Matrix

Matrix organisations are almost always organisations with several different types of professional or managerial disciplines. They stress teamwork, particularly across functional and departmental boundaries. This means that there is more than one line of accountability in managerial terms. The staff member may be accountable to one manager for certain professional tasks (eg social work) and accountable to another manager for, say, area responsibilities. There is often tension between the different disciplines. This will be viewed as worthwhile on balance in meeting the overall goal of empowering staff. In this environment, strategic planning can be misunderstood as a desire for centralisation rather than a tool or technique for necessary future direction.

Federal

A federal organisation exists where a group of voluntary organisations undertaking a series of activities serving a particular user group (eg Age Concern for the elderly) have come together to establish a superstructure, often at national or regional level, for limited common purposes. The regional constituent organisations retain substantial autonomy, while the federal organisation acts as a spokesperson and often provides services. The location of power and the nature of organisational politics are particularly important in federal organisations approaching strategic planning.

Role bureaucracy

The environment of the bureaucracy is the opposite of that of the simple structure: stable but complex. The complexity means that tasks need to be carried out by well-trained staff. The stability means that these tasks, especially the skills required, can be standardised. The role bureaucracy is likely to be most concerned with how strategy affects efficiency. The role bureaucracy is unlikely to change direction swiftly and will find the shift to a more entrepreneurial outlook difficult. Organisations with this structure tend to have a role culture.

Exercise 8   Diagnosing your organisation's structure

Think about the descriptions of the six types of structure given above. Which is closest to your own organisation's structure?

Decentralisation

The pressure of change brings with it a strategic choice – whether to decentralise or to centralise.

Example – decentralisation

The massive growth of the National Schizophrenia Fellowship (NSF) since 1990 and developments in community care have been major factors in prompting a policy decision to undertake a major drive for decentralisation. The additional pressures that have led the NSF to decentralise have been the complexity of its work, the need to stimulate local activity, the commitment to campaigning on behalf of its target group, and funding opportunities. The process of decentralisation has been at the heart of the organisation's strategy.

The process of decentralisation has brought some countervailing pressures. In response to these, the organisation has tightened national quality assurance procedures to guarantee high standards. The requirements for planning and monitoring by the centre have grown. The need for monitoring has been met by a social audit to ensure that the organisation is meeting the needs of the most severely mentally ill.

The process of continuing decentralisation has required NSF to address management issues with major strategic implications. One such issue is the level at which expenditure should be authorised for specific budgets and items. Another concerns the division of fundraising costs between the centre and the regions. The accounting arrangements have changed so that the regions are now charged management fees.

Exercise 9   Thinking about decentralisation

Think about the NSF example. Which pressures might it have experienced that would have slowed or halted its move to decentralisation?

Our list is:

- hostile environment
- constitutional issues about the ability to devolve
- claims that vital knowledge had to be safeguarded at the centre
- irresponsibility or lack of knowledge in local offices or branches
- views of donors and registering authorities
- danger of internal dissension thus alienating donors
- expense of contacting members
- time, effort and cost of liaison and co-ordination

Tools and techniques

Many of the techniques we are about to describe may seem unfamiliar at first glance. Closer examination may show that you have used part of the technique for other purposes. Our experience is that voluntary organisations use a relatively narrow range of strategic planning techniques. This section will help to broaden the range of tools you can use.

SWOT analysis

The first technique we want to introduce you to is SWOT analysis – Strengths, Weaknesses, Opportunities, Threats. This is probably the best known technique in business and strategic planning. We will be using it again in Chapter 5. SWOT is recognised as a good way to organise and summarise the internal and external position of your organisation. The simplest way to do the analysis is to take a large piece of paper and draw two lines across the centre, one vertically and one horizontally, so that it is divided into four quarters. Head these spaces 'Strengths', 'Weaknesses', 'Opportunities' and 'Threats'. Fill in on the diagram words and phrases applicable to your organisation under each heading.

The definition of the purpose of the SWOT analysis will influence the outcome. The more tightly defined the purpose, the more likely it is that the SWOT analysis will be informative and insightful for your organisation. For example, one of your objectives might be to offer live music groups as a promoter and you want to compare yourselves with the competition. It is well to think not only of other people's concerts but of the attractions of other entertainers, and of the choice for the consumer of staying at home with a CD.

How does the SWOT analysis affect the strategy of an organisation? It allows you to identify the factors that will contribute most to success. Make sure that you include your values in the assessment. It allows you to compare where you are now with where you want to be. This does not always mean that environmental conditions will allow you to get where you want to in the short term.

SWOT originated in marketing but is widely used in management, including some large national voluntary organisations. If it is to work it calls for a degree of honesty that can frankly be painful or at least difficult at times. It also calls for research and information.

Strengths and weaknesses are primarily internal. Opportunities and threats are primarily external. Strengths and weaknesses are about where the organisation is now. Opportunities and threats are about where the organisation is going.

For the purpose of the SWOT analysis, opportunities are attractive arenas for action where the organisation is likely to have some advantage or special contribution. Threats are unfavourable trends or specific disturbances in the environment that could lead to stagnation, decline or demise of the organisation or a part of it.

SWOT analysis can be undertaken in different ways. It can be done on an individual basis. It may also be done on a group basis, brainstorming points in a 'round robin' to produce an initial list. Brainstorming is covered in more detail in Appendix 1.

If you use the SWOT technique keep the results, particularly for use with Chapter 5. If you have already done a SWOT analysis, try again and compare the two; the differences can be illuminating.

The act of doing the SWOT analysis itself can release a lot of energy. Finding the weaknesses may be easiest but uncovering the strengths is often exciting once the process has gained momentum. However, SWOT analyses can be open to bias, subjectivity, unwarranted optimism, an overgenerous selection of strengths and too limited a selection of weaknesses. It is helpful to decide before carrying out the brainstorming whether it will be followed by a discussion that critically evaluates the list of points drawn up. Some examples of SWOT analyses are given below.

PEST

Where should you look for opportunities and threats? A full external assessment will include any changes there are in the Political, Economic, Social and Technological environment that will affect your organisation – this is called a PEST or STEP analysis depending on which order you prefer to put the letters in.

Examples – the value of PEST

Somalia

A deteriorating human rights situation in Somalia has been the trigger for organisations and agencies (eg social services, the police, etc) concerned with meeting refugee needs in the UK to make contact with Somali welfare organisations and prepare contingency plans for receiving refugees.

Antarctica

A Women's Institute branch resolution on preserving Antarctica alerted the National Federation of Women's Institutes (NFWI) to the long-term environmental threat. It got a two-thirds majority at the NFWI AGM, and the federation then joined forces with the World Wide Fund for Nature and Greenpeace to lobby government.

For many voluntary organisations, PEST will involve reviewing the relationship with the agencies of central government, local government, the National Health Service (NHS) and other public service agencies. It is also the opportunity to assess frankly your relationships with corporate bodies. Ask yourself how these relationships might be in one year's time, three years' time and five years' time.

PEST links to the opportunities and threats part of a SWOT analysis in pressing you to consider what changes you can expect in your immediate environment. Most importantly, these are likely to include changes in the views and interests of stakeholders, whether users, funders or collaborators, and indeed how your competitors might react to changes in the immediate environment. Following the 1992 Charities Act, for example, the Youth Hostel Association realised that it would need to change its legal status.

You may find all these questions easy to answer. If on the other hand you do not, you may need to devote some energy regularly to this type of environmental scanning. Having done this, you will probably want to:

- track the development of any trends you have observed
- make projections of their likely future direction
- assess how the changes will affect the strategy and strategic planning of your organisation.

This may require you to change your systems for collecting data.

Examples – SWOT

Royal Victoria Dock Water Sports Centre
Royal Victoria Dock Water Sports Centre is a trust located in the Docklands area of the London Borough of Newham in the East End of London. Here is the list of strengths and weaknesses it has developed.

Strengths
- Low cost outdoor watersports in acknowledged deprived geographical area.
- Available to all sections of the community, youth and adults with ethos of fostering wider community co-operation.

- Provides scope for personal development and participation through exciting sporting activities.
- Expert instruction/tuition in sports.
- Staff with professional approach and low turnover.
- Only watersports facility in the borough.
- Excellent summer scheme.
- Very visible activities.
- Strong voluntary support, particularly from local youth.
- Employment and training opportunities for local people, especially youth.
- Allows achievement of a nationally recognised sporting qualification.
- Large increases in use since inception.
- Breaks down barriers to sports previously seen as elitist.
- Flexible service delivery.

Weaknesses
- Lacks resources to develop excellence in sport.
- Heavy reliance on outside funding.
- Project needs considerable funding that cannot be met from user base.
- No permanent accommodation.
- Lack of security of tenure on premises.
- Lacks resources to consistently reach all minority cultural groups, older people and disabled people.
- Constricted budget.
- Poorly accessible transport.
- Lack of capital for equipment maintenance and replacement – overall quality of craft quite poor.

YHA
When the Youth Hostel Association became more market driven in the early 1980s, it decided that it wanted to assess its position in the family market. This was the analysis that it made:

Strengths	Weaknesses
Price	Variable product
Social benefits	No daytime access
Choice of self-catering or meals	Family rooms not
High repeat business	guaranteed
Locations	Limited/basic facilities
	Shortage of suitable
	accommodation at
	peak times and in key
	places

Opportunities	Threats
Develop specific family hostels	Seasonality
Include family provision within	Low cost competition
specific development programme	with better facilities
Create full day access	
Improve booking procedures	
Review pricing	
Improve/standardise facilities	
Promote more actively	

Readers who are keen hikers and ramblers might like to consider what points they would want to add to this analysis as users of youth hostels.

Portfolio analysis

Many voluntary organisations have more than one significant activity. Portfolio analysis allows organisations to consider whether they have the right activities in their portfolio. It is particularly relevant to the position of service provider organisations and can be useful for voluntary organisations which are severely constrained in the activities they undertake. Activities may have been taken on at the request of a funder, or it may be difficult in the short term for some organisations to extract themselves from certain activities or commitments. Even in these cases, you can examine whether the current levels of activity and pattern of resource allocation within the present portfolio should be maintained.

Portfolio analysis maps and relates two factors (see Figure 3). The first is how attractive the activity is to the outside world, external attractiveness. The second is how appropriate the activity is to the organisation itself, internal appropriateness. The tools of 'experience curve benefit' and 'life cycle of need' provided later in this chapter can assist you in mapping these factors.

The issues affecting external attractiveness include:

- level and trend of public and political support
- ability to attract resources, whether money, publicity for the cause, or volunteers
- user response

The issues affecting internal appropriateness include:

- experience with the activity
- expertise
- position on these two points in relation to other organisations
- contribution to your mission and objectives

Figure 3 Portfolio Analysis

		Internal Appropriateness	
	High	Moderate	Low
High			
External Attractiveness Moderate			
Low			

The closer an activity is to the top left-hand corner of Figure 3, the more it is to be encouraged. The closer it is to the bottom right-hand corner, the more likely it is that the resources which that activity uses can be better employed elsewhere.

Trends over time are also relevant. An activity currently in the bottom right might be worth continuing if you could see it moving towards the top left before too long. One possible development of this model is to plot activities that you are not yet doing to see where they fit.

Exercise 10 Portfolio analysis

Carry out three portfolio analyses in a form similar to that given in Figure 3. Do one for your organisation as it is now, then a second for where you were five years ago and a third for where you believe you will be in five years' time.

What does this exercise indicate for your organisation's present and future strategy?

Experience curve benefits

In the private sector, a relationship has been noted between the total amount of a product that has been produced and the unit costs of production. The growing experience in producing the product causes the costs to fall over time. This is of interest to voluntary organisations in delivering services in terms of the total resource committed. This is particularly true of those who operate in a contract culture environment.

The distinctive competence that some voluntary organisations built up in the 1980s in managing and developing employment training schemes is an example of an experience curve benefit. The benefit could be measured in organisational costs, staff and volunteer experience, and quality of service to and by the trainees. Figure 4 illustrates this concept.

Figure 4 Experience curve benefits

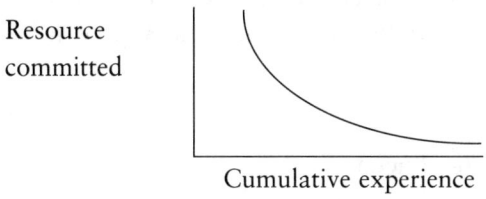

Cumulative experience

Exercise 11 Experience curve benefits

Does your organisation enjoy any experience curve benefits? If it does, work out where it is on an experience curve for a major service or activity. Has it realised all the benefits that it might have from its experience? How long is that experience valid for?

As the last question in the exercise suggested, there are important limitations to the experience curve. These lie in the rapidly changing demands of users, the shifting priorities of funders, and the dangers of being strapped into one overriding method of operation because of some short-term advantages.

The experience curve can nevertheless assist you in working out the internal appropriateness of your present and future portfolio of activities. It can help to project the level of effort or endeavour necessary to obtain the quality of service, product or action required. The loss of experience curve benefits has to be considered as a cost of a radical change from activities that are already well established.

Life cycle of need

Many voluntary organisations are driven by user needs. While some of these needs are relatively stable, others are not. The life cycle of a need plots how the level of demand arising from that need will change over time. The growth of organisations specialising in HIV and Aids in the last ten years is a result of a rising life cycle of need. Assessing this can help to determine the external attractiveness of your organisation in portfolio analysis. Ideas as well as needs may have such life cycles.

Example – life cycle of need

In the next ten years, we will see a significant increase in the number of people aged 85 and over. The needs of this section of the population are also growing with greatly increased demands for new and varied services. On the other hand, the attention paid to the effects of polio has fortunately declined over the twentieth century after the discovery of a vaccine.

Action points

- Describe your organisation's culture.
- Establish which structural form you are closest to.
- Do a SWOT analysis.
- Undertake a portfolio analysis for your organisation.
- Establish which experience curve benefits you have or could enjoy.

Chapter 4
A Sense of Purpose

This chapter helps you to establish, agree and formalise a sense of purpose. It explains the components of purpose: values, mission and vision.

Chapters 1 and 2 have explained how critical purpose is in a volatile world. It acts as a touchstone that organisations can use to gauge whether they are doing the right thing. Some organisations believe that if their purpose is clear enough, the resources will materialise to allow them to carry it out. The process of developing the mission statement is also good for both clarity and consensus. It helps all stakeholders, but especially staff, to gain a sense of identity.

What is purpose?

There are three components of purpose: values, mission and vision. What do these terms mean?

- *Values* are the 'how': what are the underlying beliefs of the organisation that decide how it behaves?
- *Mission* is the 'why': why does the organisation exist? What is its *raison d'être* or reason for being?
- *Vision* is the 'what': what is the picture of success?

In other publications or settings you may find either that some of these words are given a slightly different meaning, or that different words are used instead. This applies especially to 'mission'; it may be given a wider meaning than here, or a phrase like 'statement of purpose' may be used to mean what 'mission' means in this book. It is not a question of one being right and another being wrong. It is rather a question of choosing a consistent set of definitions that best fits the task in hand.

The three components of purpose are now considered in more detail. For each, the following questions are answered:

- What is it for?
- How important is it for an organisation?
- How do you produce a written statement?

The procedures described in this chapter are mostly for groups, who will need to be led through them. You will want to decide whether to act as facilitator yourself, use someone else from within the organisation, or use an outsider.

We strongly recommend that you tackle the three components in the order in which they are covered here.

Values

Values are things that people think have value or worth. They may be beliefs, attitudes or principles. They act as the glue that binds the members of the organisation together. To share at least a few core values is essential.

Many voluntary organisations have evolved a common set of values without ever spelling them out. However, formally agreeing a common set of values has many benefits. The examples which follow illustrate these benefits, both within an organisation and in dealing with the outside world. The final example shows the importance of shared values in a volatile world.

Examples – values

Polden Puckham Charitable Trust
The Polden Puckham Charitable Trust is a recent amalgamation

of two small family trusts. On amalgamation, they set down their values for the first time. Only then did they realise that, for example, some of their investments did not match with those values.

Women's health project

A women's health project in York was having difficulty in deciding how to allocate priorities between the various ways in which it could develop its services. Making explicit their value of 'empowerment' gave them a touchstone and enabled them to make choices.

Quicks

Quicks is a South London commercial stationery supplier. The four members of the Quick family who run the business are born-again Christians. They tried to employ Christians, but as a result spent months trying unsuccessfully to recruit an operations manager. Also, both Christian and non-Christian employees felt wary of discussing religion, so were unsure how the directors' beliefs affected the business.

The solution was to make their values explicit, in a non-denominational code of ethics. This allows the directors to employ the candidate best qualified for the job, without worrying about his or her religious beliefs. The Quicks have separated their roles as directors and shareholders, and in the latter capacity they can continue to choose Christian causes to donate their dividends to. This approach, the Quicks feel, has resolved the tension they had previously felt between their business and religious lives.

Johnson and Johnson

Johnson and Johnson, an American health and household products group, has a statement of values called its 'Credo'. Its first line is, 'We believe our first responsibility is to the doctors, nurses, and patients, to mothers and all others who use our products and services.' Thousands of employees were involved in its development over several years. As a result staff at Johnson and Johnson reacted quickly and openly when, in 1982, a small batch of its Tylenol painkillers was maliciously poisoned. The end result was that customer trust rose, not fell.

There are dangers in developing a statement of values. Members of some organisations may share only the values needed to do the job and disagree on other values. An exercise that brought all values to the surface might then cause unnecessary disagreement. The statement must also be lived out in practice. Few things can do more damage to the faith of staff in management than to see managers not living by the values they have proclaimed. This is especially likely if the values are those the organisation thinks that it ought to have, rather than those that it actually does have.

Exercise 12 Identifying values

Values are difficult to identify and easy to confuse with objectives, for example. The stated values of one organisation are listed below. Do you think that all of them are actually values?

- radical
- influential
- visionary
- successful
- professional
- having integrity
- empowering

Possible answer: 'successful' sounds like an objective.

'Influential' could be an objective, or it could be a value, a belief that results should be achieved by influencing others, rather than directly.

Constructing a statement of values

The first step in constructing a values statement is to list what you think are your organisation's values. If you find it difficult to identify your values, you can go through the organisation's literature and pick out the values expressed in it. Below is an example from a briefing on ecofeminism published by the Women's Environmental Network (WEN). The words that appear to be values are in italics.

Example – identifying values

WEN

> WEN takes a *radical* approach to environmentalism, searching for long-term solutions rather than short-term political compromises and viewing environmental problems *holistically* in global context rather than in a reductionist and isolated manner . . . WEN's ecofeminist philosophy elevates the feminine aspect of *intuition* to its rightful place as a leading mechanism for life preservation . . . WEN seeks to fulfil its ecofeminist philosophy in aiming both to facilitate a greater understanding for many women of their relationship to their environment and to *empower* many women to act.

There are several different sorts of values here. To 'empower' is a principle, relating to what WEN does. 'Radical' and a holistic approach are also principles, but relate to how the organisation acts. 'Intuition' is a human characteristic to which WEN gives particular value.

'Environmentalism' may or may not be a value. It depends whether the word is being used to denote the value placed on the environment, or the activity that value to which leads.

The second step is to pick out the key values. Here is an example of a list from Emergency Exit Arts, a firework theatre group:

- initiate new work
- be valued and value ourselves
- break barriers
- nourish personal growth and development
- respect and enable creativity
- value both the process and the product
- be challenging

The third step is to review the list. Questions to ask might include:

- What is the relationship between the values? Are they all consistent? If not, what does that say about the organisation? Do some of the values support a more fundamental value? Suppose 'co-operation' had been listed. Thinking about the purpose of co-operation might reveal that the underlying value was 'harmony', and that this was a better word.
- Is it possible to tell whether the organisation is living out each of these values? If so, what is the evidence? If it is not living them out, what would it look like if it did so?

Finally the agreed list of values can be turned into a statement. This is usually best done by one person initially and then discussed by the planning team.

Example – values statement

Metropolitan Police
This statement from the Metropolitan Police starts with the 'what' of the mission and ends with the 'how' of values.

> The purpose of the Metropolitan Police Service is to uphold the law fairly and firmly; to prevent crime; to pursue and bring to justice those who break the law; to keep The Queen's Peace; to protect, help and reassure people in London; and to be seen to do all this with integrity, common sense and sound judgement.

We must be compassionate, courteous and patient, acting without fear or favour or prejudice to the rights of others. We need to be professional, calm and restrained in the face of violence and apply only that force which is necessary to accomplish our lawful duty.

We must strive to reduce the fears of the public and, so far as we can, to reflect their priorities in the action we take. We must respond to well-founded criticism with a willingness to change.

Exercise 13 Constructing a statement of values

This is an exercise for the planning team.

1 Make a list of your organisation's values. This can be done individually or in groups of three to six people. Make one person responsible for collecting all the contributions and putting together an overall list.

2 Divide into groups of three to six people. Give each group a copy of the consolidated list of values and five postcards (or Post-It notes). Allow the groups about half an hour to select what they consider to be the five most important values and write one on each card, numbering them from 1 to 5 with 1 signifying the most important.

3 Pin the cards (or stick the notes) on a board or wall. Bring the members of the planning team together and give them time to discuss the selections and make a final list.

4 Review the final list as a group to identify any inconsistencies and relationships, and whether the values are being upheld.

5 Develop a values statement based on the final list. Depending on your organisation's culture, it may be best to designate one person to do this, or you may want to produce different statements, either individually or in small groups, and then consolidate them as you did with the lists of values.

Mission

An organisation needs to agree its reason for existing, its mission, in order to be effective. Clarity and consensus on the mission are so important that it must be written down, even if it is not made available outside the organisation.

Example – mission statements

NEEC
The Nisga'a is an Indian nation of 6,000 people in north-western British Columbia, Canada. When the Nisga'a Economic Enterprises Corporation (NEEC) tried to produce a mission statement, each of three groups produced a different mission. The three versions were:

- Investor in and owner of businesses.
- Technical advice and training for businesses.
- Doing research and providing information.

As a result, 'We realised that nobody was really clear what business NEEC was supposed to be in. No wonder it had been so ineffective!'

A mission statement should try to meet several different criteria. It should say:

- why the organisation exists
- what the organisation does; by implication it should also make clear what the organisation does not do
- for whom the organisation exists
- anything else that makes the organisation unique or special

The mission statement should be:

- clear
- brief and memorable

- inspiring
- demanding but achievable
- workable
- stable

There are of course trade-offs implicit in these criteria. The need for brevity, for example, is in conflict with the need to spell out what the organisation does and does not do.

Most organisations will tend to emphasise one out of 'why', 'what' and 'for whom'. The names of these three organisations, for example, show their emphasis immediately:

- Centre for Creation Spirituality (why)
- The Barnes Workhouse Fund (what)
- War Amputations of Canada (for whom)

If there is a choice between describing a process and an output, use the output. For example, the mission of a teacher education faculty college is not the process of training, but the output of trained teachers.

It is vital to be clear. Below is a completely unclear mission statement, with a second version that suddenly reveals what the organisation is all about.

Before
- Improve people's quality of life through the creative design and development of devices to eliminate the unsafe presence of certain undesirable species.

After
- Design and develop mouse traps.

Stability is an equally important feature. If the mission statement is completely revised every couple of years, it cannot be describing the fundamental purpose of the organisation. On the other hand, it is very difficult to get a mission right first time, and it may be several years before you feel completely comfortable with it.

Some missions are so specific that you can tell whether and when they have been achieved. This has advantages and disadvantages. Both are illustrated by the case of the US space agency, NASA. J F Kennedy set the following mission for NASA in 1960: 'To put a man on the moon in ten years'. It then looked all but impossible. The mission statement, being so concrete, was a very powerful motivator, and the mission was achieved in 1969. But once it was achieved it had no force, and NASA has not been so targeted in its activities since then.

It is important to remember that different people may have divergent views about why their organisation exists. There is a story of three medieval stonecutters in a quarry who were asked what they were doing. The first said, 'I'm cutting stone.' The second said, 'I'm building a cathedral.' The third said, 'I'm glorifying God.' Taking these as mission statements for the individuals concerned, they become successively less clear and further removed from the job itself, but much more inspiring.

Some mission statements become more widely defined over time. The Barnes Workhouse Fund still exists, but it no longer funds workhouses. The Brooke Hospital for Animals was originally intended to deal with army horses remaining in Egypt after the war of 1914–1918. It soon evolved into a provider of veterinary services for the horses owned by locals. Taking a commercial example, British Rail would until recently have thought of itself as being in the transport business. Now, teleconferencing is an alternative to travelling to meetings by train. In this respect British Rail could think of itself as being in the business of communications, and this may bring about a wider definition of its mission.

Examples – mission statements

NFWI

The National Federation of Women's Institutes (NFWI) took over a year to develop its mission. Consultation with its members produced 1,500 responses. From those, words and phrases that recurred were used to help develop the following statement:

> The Women's Institute offers opportunities for all women
> to enjoy friendship
> to learn
> to widen their horizons
> and together
> to influence
> local, national and international affairs

From the mission statement the Federation developed a slogan, 'Today's women working for tomorrow's world'. It uses both mission statement and slogan on its promotional material.

Compare the mission statement with the statement of aims below, quoted in the 1991 annual report. The two are closely related, but the mission is far more punchy.

The WI aims to . . .

- improve and develop the quality of life, particularly in rural areas
- advance the education of women in citizenship and in public issues, national and international
- enable women to work together through the WI to put into practice the ideals for which the organisation stands

The Royal National Lifeboat Institute (RNLI)

> The preservation of life from shipwreck

This mission statement is very crisp and satisfies almost all the criteria. It perhaps does not say how the RNLI preserves life. For example, does it use helicopters in addition to lifeboats?

Girl Scouts of America

> To help a girl reach her highest potential

The Girl Scouts have found this very helpful in deciding what not to do. They have rejected opportunities that do not relate to the mission. These included supporting women's rights activists and working with other charities that wanted to use the Scouts' door-to-door canvassing organisation.

A Catholic religious order

> To engage, under the standard of the Cross, in the crucial struggle for faith and that struggle for justice which it includes

As well as being brief, this statement draws on earlier statements of purpose; in this case, the earlier statements go back to the sixteenth century. This lends a sense of continuity to the mission.

The World Wide Fund for Nature (WWF)

Below are three different statements. Note that although the wording for those in 1978 and in 1986 looks similar at first glance, there is a crucial difference. By 1986 the emphasis on endangered species had gone. This corresponds with WWF's change of name from the World Wildlife Fund in 1988.

One potential problem with these particular statements is that words like 'maximum' ('to raise the maximum funds possible') or 'best' make it impossible to tell whether the mission is really being achieved.

> **1978**
> To raise the maximum funds possible from UK sources and to ensure that the funds are used wisely for the benefit of conservation of renewable natural resources, with emphasis on endangered species and habitats.

> **1986**
> To raise the maximum funds possible from UK sources and to ensure that these funds are used wisely for the benefit of conservation of renewable natural resources, in accordance with the principles of the World Conservation Strategy.

> **1989**
> To achieve the conservation of nature and ecological processes by:

- Preserving genetic, species and ecosystem diversity
- Ensuring that the use of renewable natural resources is sustainable both now and in the longer term, for the benefit of all life on earth
- Promoting actions to reduce, to a minimum, pollution and the wasteful exploitation and consumption of resources and energy

The New Economics Foundation (NEF)

1988
The New Economics Foundation exists to develop and promote a flexible economics which will lead to a high and sustainable quality of life for all.

1993
To develop and promote new economic approaches which can help build an economy that is sustainable, socially just and able to deliver a high quality of life for all.

These two statements show a slow evolution. Note that both versions are weak on 'what' and 'for whom'. They fail the criterion of clarity – the word 'help' is vague and sets no boundaries, so does nothing to say what NEF does not do. It could usefully be replaced by whatever main tasks constitute the help.

Traidcraft

To establish a just trading system which expresses the principles of love and justice fundamental to the Christian faith.

Note that the more a mission envisages an end result, as here, the closer it becomes to being a vision, discussed in the next section.

Magic Me

Magic Me aims to provide education and encourage awareness about issues of ageing and citizenship. To achieve this it aims:

- to give young and older people an opportunity to improve their confidence and self esteem and thus be more in control of their lives
- to create a sense of community through encouraging shared creative activity and interaction between young and older people
- to complement, challenge and enrich the work of institutions and services which have an impact on the lives of young and older people (particularly residential homes and schools) and the staff who work in and manage them.

This statement represents a mission rather than a vision, since Magic Me believes that it is achieving its mission at present. It accompanies the above statement with a statement of the attested benefits that participants receive.

Exercise 14 Evaluating a mission statement

Before attempting to devise your own mission statement, it can be helpful to try to evaluate one from another organisation. Read the mission statement below, from the Blackfriars Settlement in London, then tackle the questions and points that follow.

Blackfriars Settlement provides resources to help meet the changing needs of the people of North Southwark and Waterloo. We aim to:

- work with local people to achieve their economic, educational and social potential
- develop project work that tackles poverty, prejudice and powerlessness
- deliver appropriate services to meet the needs of the area
- foster active partnership with individuals, community groups, public services and the private sector

1 Does the statement make it clear why the organisation exists?

2 Underline the parts that describe what the organisation does.

3 Circle the parts that describe for whom the organisation exists.

4 How many other of our criteria does the statement meet?

Possible answers to questions 1 and 4

1 On the whole, yes. This is the Settlement's first attempt at a mission statement and there are two areas that could perhaps be tightened up. The first is the needs of the people for whom the Settlement exists. We can deduce that the need is to 'tackle poverty, prejudice and powerlessness' in order to 'achieve their economic, educational and social potential'. But it is not clear whether this is complete. The second area is the contribution that the Settlement will make. How will it help? It is difficult to tell what the Settlement is not going to do, and so difficult to tell what it will do.

4 It sounds demanding but achievable and workable. It is not brief, which hampers its ability to be memorable and inspiring. There is no obvious reason why it should not be stable.

Exercise 15 Developing a mission statement

There are two stages to this exercise. The first is for the planner to do. It is intended to provide background information for the second stage in an organisation where there is no existing mission statement, although you might want to do it even when a statement does exist. The second stage is designed as a group exercise.

Stage 1 – Planner

1 Find as many descriptions of your organisation's mission as you can. This may be the statement of charitable objectives, descriptions in brochures, funding applications, and so on.

2 Pick out from the material you have collected the elements that best achieve each of the criteria for a mission statement listed above.

3 Combine the elements into a rough and ready mission statement. Don't worry about getting the language right at this stage. You can use this as a point of comparison with the draft statements produced in Stage 2, but don't read it to the group before the members have written their versions since you want to avoid influencing their thinking.

Stage 2 – Group exercise
Requirements: felt-tip pens; several sheets of flipchart paper attached to the walls.

1 Explain to the group what a mission statement is and why it is important. Run through the criteria listed above, stressing especially the first four – why, what, for whom, and what makes the organisation special.

2 Ask everyone to construct a mission statement of their own. Tell them to concern themselves only with content, not with grammar and style. Then ask them to write their statements on the flipchart paper. Allow 20–30 minutes for this part of the exercise.

3 Give everyone the opportunity to read their statement aloud to the group. Discourage comments at this stage.

4 Lead the group in consolidating the statements. It may help to take 'why', 'what' and 'for whom' in turn, and to start with the one that seems most fundamental to the organisation. Look for ideas or for phrases that appeal to the group as a whole, or at least to most of it. Write these ideas and phrases up on the flipchart paper.

5 Help the group to complete a sentence beginning, 'The mission of the (name of organisation) is . . .' Test the result against our criteria. If it still seems vague, asking the question 'So what?' should clarify the benefit you are offering to users.

6 The effort to be comprehensive may mean that the mission statement is too long to be easily remembered. You may want to do a further exercise, on this occasion or later on, to produce a condensed version that is short and memorable. This can be attempted individually and the results consolidated, or done collectively from the outset. It may help to try to reduce your mission to three words – although you may need to allow yourself a few more.

Example – memorable missions

The Red Cross managed to condense its lengthy mission to 'Care in Crisis'. And remember the Women's Institute's slogan: 'Today's women working for tomorrow's world'.

Do not assume that your charitable objectives will serve as a mission statement, except as a starting point. They are often widely drawn, are vague about priorities, and give no sense of a time frame. Here for example are the core charitable objectives of the Bible Lands Society, widely used on their notepaper and in their literature:

> A fellowship of Christians united in the common aim of helping Christian mission in the lands of the Bible especially the Holy Land in the work of carrying the Gospel back to the lands of its birth and in providing comfort, education and healing for the sick, blind, disabled, poor and homeless.

On the other hand, you cannot do anything that is not in your charitable objectives. The Brooke Hospital for Animals, for instance, cannot open clinics for horses in Spain, because its sphere of operation is restricted to the Middle East and the Indian subcontinent.

Mission statements are difficult to get right. It helps to have the views of people not involved in the group exercise, which will also increase ownership in the wider organisation. In order to find out these views you have to allow time for drafts to be circulated and comments collected, which can be a lengthy process in a large organisation. The NFWI took over a year to develop its mission in consultation with its members.

Furthermore, although mission statements should last for several years, you may not feel that you have got yours right first time. You may want to come back to it in a year or two and review it in the light of experience. Some of the examples given above illustrate this kind of evolution.

Exercise 16 How likely are you to achieve your mission?

Whereas the rest of the exercises in this chapter are based on achieving consensus, this exercise draws out different opinions. If many members of your planning team do not consider that your mission is likely to be achieved, it may be wise to review whether that is the correct mission for your organisation. First read the description of force field analysis in Appendix 1.

1 Ask each member of the team to write down what he or she estimates as the percentage chance of the organisation achieving its mission. (You may need to specify a time period for achievement.)

2 Plot the results on a line stretching from 0 per cent to 100 per cent, putting names against the appropriate percentage. Work out the average percentage and mark it on the line.

3 Discuss why people have reached their particular estimates. Use the results in a force field analysis.

4 Keep the results of the analysis for use when you are planning the implementation of your strategy.

Be aware that it is possible for subunits of an organisation to set their own mission statements, usually derived from the overall mission. Doing this may help to ease any conflicts of opinion, but be watchful for conflicting values which could affect the way the organisation as a whole is perceived.

Vision

It is not essential to have a vision. An organisation can be effective in the short term without knowing where it wants to be in the long term. But it will be more effective if it has in mind a vision of future success. US companies with a vision are said to have been 50 times more successful than those without a vision, based on their share prices since the 1920s.

Example – vision

Visions in British voluntary organisations are hard to find, so this example comes from the Nisga'a, an Indian nation in Canada. This is the first part of their vision (illustrated in Figure 5):

We have a vision of ourselves inhabiting our homeland, Nisga'a people and communities nourished and sustained by the wealth of the Niss Valley and in turn exercising our rights and responsibility to care for and protect the land.

We have a vision of our children's children describing the homeland in the Nisga'a language, celebrating our relationship to the land through our cultural traditions and art. We have a vision of our children's children confidently using the most modern technology to manage the land and communicate with those we relate to and trade with in the larger society.

Of the three components of purpose, a vision is probably the most powerful motivator. Think what the vision of Nirvana has done for Buddhism, or what the vision of heaven has done for Christianity.

This is how two powerful people explain how a sense of vision can motivate people:

Those who anticipate the future are empowered to create it.

John F Kennedy

If you want to move people, it has to be toward a vision that's positive for them, that taps important values, that gets them something they desire, and it has to be presented in a compelling way that they feel inspired to follow.

Martin Luther King

Figure 5 The Nisga'a Vision

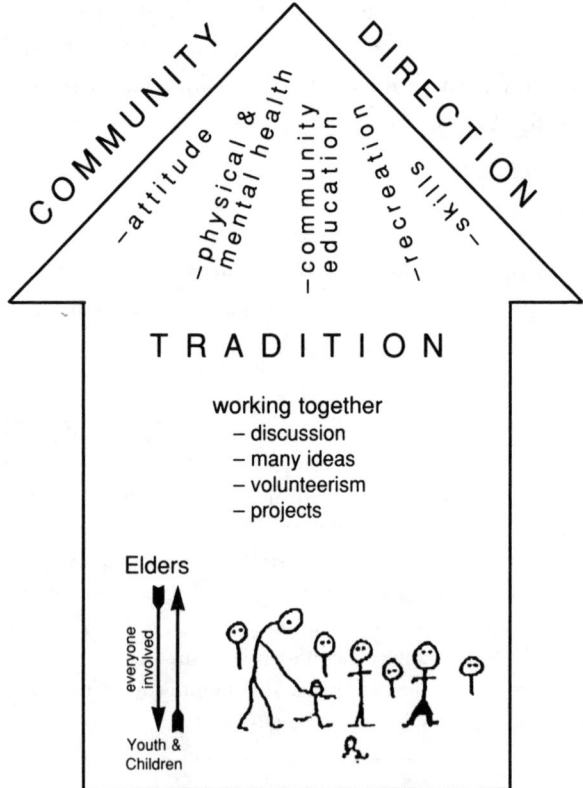

These visions are all visions for society at large. Visions may also be intended for an organisation. These two types of vision are very different. Where there is a particular wrong to be put right, the vision of success for the organisation will be its own dissolution. This is difficult to contemplate, but healthy if you can achieve it.

A vision is especially difficult to formulate in the early life of an organisation. If people have come together to tackle an urgent short-term need, they may at first have no agreement on the longer term. It may take several years for this to develop.

Example – delaying a vision

When the Post Office was trying to change its culture in the late 1980s, it took the conscious decision to delay developing a vision for some years. In the words of the manager in charge of quality, 'People would have said, "that's not us". They always felt that the Royal Mail was so special.'

The criteria for an effective vision are that it should:

- provide a challenge for the whole organisation
- reflect the values and the mission statement
- be realistic, simple and clear
- be able to be translated into goals and strategies

Exercise 17 Creating a vision

1 Divide the planning team into groups of three to six people. Ask each group to develop an answer to the questions: 'What is your vision of what you want our organisation and the world we work in to look like in 5, 10 or 20 years' time? What are its key features?' Emphasise that you want an ideal view, which does not have to take account of the present. Provide flipchart paper and felt-tip pens, and encourage

people to express themselves in whatever way seems appropriate. Allow 1–1½ hours for this part of the exercise.

2 Bring the team together and ask each group to present its vision to the others. Allow questions only for clarification.

3 Ask everyone to identify and comment on similarities and differences between the various visions. Emphasise that there is no right or wrong answer.

4 Either produce a consolidated version as a group or designate one person to do this after the meeting.

5 You may find it helpful to return to your small groups to identify the key obstacles to achieving the vision. List separately the obstacles inside and outside the organisation. The results can then be discussed in the larger group.

Visualisation

Visualisation is a technique which can be useful in developing a vision. It will appeal to people who are primarily visual, and may draw extra ideas out of everybody because it taps the unconscious mind. Two approaches are described below to be used with groups; an experienced facilitator would help you to gain the most benefit from the technique.

First approach
- Ask everyone to find a comfortable position, sitting or standing.
- Ask everyone to close their eyes and relax. To encourage them, you could ask them to remember a time when they felt relaxed and happy, or imagine a place of peace, or just feel heaviness sinking through them and out into the ground.
- Ask people to allow an image of the organisation as it is now to emerge in their mind. They should not censor – the image does not have to 'make sense'.

- Ask people to draw the image, in whatever way suits them, without worrying about the quality of the drawing.
- Repeat the visualisation for the organisation in the future – it will probably help to specify how far in the future.
- Pin the drawings up on the wall and discuss as a group what similarities and differences are apparent.

Second approach
- Encourage everyone to relax as described above.
- Now ask people to visualise the future of the organisation. Here are three ways of doing this – others may occur to you.
  - Imagine you are watching a film of the progress of the organisation over the years to come.
  - Imagine you are at a great height, possibly on a mountain top, looking down on the organisation several years in the future.
  - Imagine you are 20 years in the future, looking back on the organisation as it will be in 10 years' time.
- Ask people to call out what they experience and to be as concrete in their descriptions as possible: ask them what they can see, hear and smell.
- Record what people say.
- At the end, bring people gently back to the present.
- Discuss the similarities and differences which emerged.

Action points

- Decide who is to act as facilitator for developing your purpose.
- Decide which procedures to use.
- Decide what background material participants should receive and provide it.
- Carry out the exercises to develop your organisation's values, mission and vision.
- Write up the results.

Chapter 5
Fitting Strategy to Purpose

Chance favours the prepared mind.
Louis Pasteur

The great German poet, Goethe, believed that the universe responds when you declare your purpose to it. This chapter is for those who warm to this optimism but would like to have done some preparation for the happy event. It guides you through the difficult middle game of strategy formulation by explaining appropriate tools and techniques. A number of these tools and techniques will be unfamiliar to the voluntary sector organisation.

These tools and techniques have two purposes. They assist the search for information and ideas, and they synthesise ideas into working generalisations and patterns, in order to develop options for the strategy. This chapter offers some alternative approaches, indicating the settings in which each will be most appropriate.

Gap analysis

Gap analysis is a useful addition to your organisation's toolkit. It considers the gap between where you are now and where you want to get to. It offers one way of identifying your position, and can help you to see how far you have progressed towards achieving your mission and vision.

Some campaigning voluntary organisations may have goals that are so all-encompassing – achieving a sustainable natural environment, for example – that they feel that gap analysis is not relevant. However, all these goals represent an illusion of reality which your organisation is not, in fact, capable of delivering. This is not to diminish the importance of the ultimate objective, but you must first identify a mission, goals and objectives that have a realistic chance of success on the way to this greater purpose.

Gap analysis can be applied for various reasons. For example, if you are an organisation which relies on member subscriptions, you may want to identify how far you have increased your membership towards your target. Or if you are a voluntary organisation specialising in child care the Children Act will have imposed additional obligations. Gap analysis can be used to estimate your gap in terms of quality thresholds, inspection requirements and staffing needs.

Exercise 18 Gap analysis

Think of your organisation in terms of the mission you have identified, or in terms of a particular issue you want to address.

1 Describe where the organisation is now.

2 Describe where you want to be by a particular date.

3 How wide is the gap between where you are and where you want to be?

4 How necessary is it that you bridge the gap?

Now that you have identified the gap, this chapter will help you to formulate a strategy for dealing with it.

Strategic staircase

It may be useful to imagine your strategy as a staircase. The staircase leads from where you are now to where you want to be. This provides a reminder that although the gap is often large, the journey is usually step by step.

In developing a strategic staircase indicating where you want to be in, say, five years' time, you are able to track back and work out in broad terms where you need to be next year. Each step involves the development of particular capabilities, skills and assets to underpin the next step the organisation wants to take. Staff and volunteers need to be able to tackle realistic, bite-sized tasks. These should be arranged to match capability and to achieve positive outcomes to raise morale.

Developing strategy can be a disturbing process when it implies significant changes for your organisation. The strategic staircase offers reassurance because it shows the end point. It builds confidence and helps people to envision the future. It also provides a practical way of taking forward the vision you developed in Chapter 4.

The staircase prompts choices between possible elements of the strategy. The choices are whether to take small steps, large steps, or to bound up the stairs. It helps to define the timetable for the strategy. As an approach the strategic staircase stresses the development of options, which may be about reduction in activities as well as growth. When the steps have been defined the strategic staircase supports the case for resources to be put behind key capabilities.

Strategic issues

So in order to develop a strategy you need to generate some strategic options. One way to do this is to focus on strategic issues. Another approach, the value chain, will be covered later in the chapter.

Backoff and Nutt, two leading US writers on management of not-for-profit organisations, define an issue as a difficulty or problem that has a significant influence on the way the organisation functions or on its ability to achieve a desired result where there is not yet an agreed response. We feel that strategic issues are best portrayed as questions about an organisational problem, capability or opportunity. The focus of the question may be internal or external or both. If there is a decision to be made, the strategic issue must be a question to which the organisation can provide some sort of answer. You will find examples of some strategic issues later in this chapter.

The advantages of the issues approach are that:

- It corresponds to the way that organisations take decisions, which is usually issue by issue.
- It corresponds to the way people feel. They usually feel strongest about particular issues rather than general concerns. Identifying these issues often makes planning seem more real.
- It prevents a rush to provide answers before the question has been properly understood.
- It directs attention to the questions that really matter.

As well as using the issues approach, strategic options can be generated by means of a value chain, which is discussed on page 95.

Following the research of John Bryson, three broad approaches can be taken to identify strategic issues – the direct approach, the goals approach, and the vision of success approach.

The direct approach

The direct approach plunges straight into identifying strategic issues. It is the best approach to take if:

- there seem to be immediate and pressing issues to which you feel you need to respond – always remember that there may be issues which are less evident but equally important;

- there is no agreement in the organisation on goals, or the goals on which there is agreement are too abstract to be useful in guiding action;
- there is no existing vision of success and developing a vision about which there is consensus will be difficult;
- there is no hierarchical authority to impose goals on the other stakeholders;
- the environment is so turbulent that you judge development of broad goals or visions to be unwise.

Given these recommendations, the direct approach works well if the organisation exists in a relatively politicised environment with a strong coalition to make things work. It is therefore particularly relevant to campaigning voluntary organisations.

Exercise 19   Using the direct approach to identify strategic issues

This is a group exercise. As background reading before the meeting, give the members of the group copies of the organisation's mission statement and the results of the SWOT analysis you carried out in Chapter 3.

1 Ask the group to name and define the strategic issues facing the organisation. This could be done by devising a series of statements beginning 'We need to . . .', intended to minimise threats and maximise opportunities. Write them up on flipchart paper and pin them on the wall.

2 Ask the group to spend some time rearranging the flipchart sheets so that similar issues are grouped together.

3 Discuss why the issues identified are *strategic* issues – how do they relate to the mission and to internal and external influences on the organisation?

4 Ask the group to evaluate how important each issue is. What would be the consequences if it were not addressed? One way to do this is to devise alternative scenarios of what might happen. For example, if the issue is 'We need to grow', the consequences might be 'if we do not grow we may be marginalised by the campaigns of other organisations'.

5 Discuss whether there are any issues that you can do nothing about, and if so, why that is the case. Keep the lists of issues to use as a basis for formulating your strategy.

The goals approach

The goals approach to identifying strategic issues begins with the organisation establishing goals and objectives for itself. Issues can then be identified which are relevant to the goals and objectives, and finally strategies developed to achieve them. While it is possible to go directly from goals to strategies, we recommend that organisations take the route of going from goals to issues to strategies. This ensures better definition of problems and opportunities and more exploration of the options available.

For the approach to work, fairly broad and deep agreement on the organisation's goals and objectives must be possible. The goals and objectives themselves must be specific and detailed enough to provide useful guidance in the development of strategies. This approach is more likely to work in organisations with hierarchical authority structures in which key decision makers can impose goals on others affected by the planning exercise. Organisations with power cultures, in particular those with few powerful stakeholders, may benefit from this approach.

Organisations with broad agendas and numerous powerful stakeholders are unlikely to achieve the kind of consensus necessary to use the goals approach effectively. An important part of the process is to ensure that the claims of different stakeholders are considered.

Exercise 20 Using the goals approach to identify strategic issues

This is a group exercise.

1 Ask members of the group to name and define strategic goals for the organisation. Write them on flipchart paper and pin them on the wall.

2 Ask the group to spend some time rearranging the flipchart sheets so that similar goals are grouped together.

3 Discuss why the goals have been identified as strategic goals.

4 Ask the group to evaluate how important each goal is. What would be the consequences if that goal were not achieved?

5 Discuss whether there are any goals that simply cannot be achieved and why that is the case. Keep the list of goals to use as a basis for formulating your strategy.

If strategic issues are identified by this exercise, they are likely to prompt such questions as:

• How do we gain the agreement of other key decision makers on this set of goals?
• How do we establish the relative priority of each of these goals?

The vision of success approach

> We ask ourselves what will the year be like? We create in our minds a visual portrait of what the economy, our industry and our company will look like. Then we move back into the present, envisioning what we have to do in small steps in order to get to the future. We call this back to the future planning.
>
> *John Scully, when President of Pepsi*

It is interesting to note the implicit use of the strategic straircase in this quotation.

In the vision of success approach to strategy identification, the organisation develops an ideal picture of itself in the future as it fulfils its mission and achieves success. The strategic issues then involve questioning how the organisation should move from the way it is now to how it should look and behave, based on its vision of success.

This approach is most useful where:

- the organisation is characterised by strong mutual support;
- it would be difficult to identify strategic issues directly;
- no goals and objectives exist and they would be difficult to develop;
- drastic change is likely to be necessary – the present may be so painful that it is easier to work back from the future;
- consensus can be achieved but it is difficult by other means to make that consensus explicit.

If you have carried out the exercise to create a vision in Chapter 4, you will already have completed some of the tasks for the vision of success approach. All that is needed here is a one-page idealised scenario of the future.

Exercise 21 Using the vision of success approach to identify strategic issues

1 Ask each member of the planning team to do the first part of this exercise on his or her own. Give them the following instructions:

- It is three years from now and your organisation has made exciting progress. It has become a recognised leader in its field. Imagine that you are a journalist detailed to write a story about the organisation. You have thoroughly reviewed the organisation's mission, staffing, financial position, organisation structure and management. Describe on no more than one side of a piece of A4 paper the main features of what you have seen.

2 Assemble as a group and ask everyone to read their reports. Note and discuss similarities and differences and the advantages and disadvantages of each vision. This discussion will identify the strategic issues facing the organisation.

Exploring issues

Now that you have identified your organisation's strategic issues, you will want to explore them in greater depth to evaluate their impact and how they might change in the future. In the past, two methods were principally employed to deal with strategic uncertainty:

- *Projecting trends forward* – this depends on the future continuing much like the past, which has ceased to be a valid assumption.
- *Forecasting* – the idea that more and more sophisticated models would somehow supply the answer has also fallen into disrepute in the face of greater complexity and volatility in the environment.

Another method that is being increasingly used is that of scenarios. Scenarios cope with uncertainty by saying not that a particular event is likely, nor that it is probable, but that it is possible. Scenarios are not a forecast or a set of numbers. They can help you to reach conclusions that run counter to your intuition, and thus challenge your mental maps of the future.

A scenario is:

- a consistent possible pattern of future development embracing political, economic, social and technological elements of change – the PEST factors introduced in Chapter 3;
- a conceptual structure into which observed events can be fitted;
- a way of exploring external issues and their prospective impact.

There are several potential benefits which come from using scenarios:

- *Avoiding being caught off guard.* Decision takers are expected to take decisions quickly and often, usually with incomplete information. They are unused to remaining uncertain and spending a lot of time exploring the future without taking decisions.

- *Recognising signs of change.* Shell had worked out by the early 1980s that if Gorbachev, then largely unknown, came to power in the USSR, there would be massive economic and political restructuring.
- *Challenging conventional views of the future.* One example of such a view was the belief held by the Hunt family of Texas that high oil price inflation in the late 1970s would continue. This did not hold true and the family lost a large chunk of its $10 billion fortune.
- *Avoiding denial.* Scenarios use the power of stories to avoid denial or other forms of blocking. Think how cinema goers willingly suspend disbelief for the sake of enjoyment!
- *Applying the reality test.* Scenarios help you understand whether strategies will work in real life. One particular radical group in South Africa announced to a conference that its strategy was to organise a workers revolution aided by the Chinese. They were challenged to describe this in the form of a scenario, as a consistent and coherent story. Trying to do so convinced not only their audience, but also themselves, that their strategy was unworkable.

Building and presenting scenarios has far more to do with art than science. Scenarios are as much about intuition as logic. The following represent the chief components in developing a scenario:

- *Identify the key issues* that the scenarios are to deal with.
- *Identify the key factors* in the local environment. What elements in your environment can affect the way your organisation conducts its business?
- *Identify the driving forces.* Which forces drive the key factors? In *Romeo and Juliet,* for example, the key forces are the romantic love between the two principals and the feud between the families.
- *Rank by importance and uncertainty.* Rank the key factors and driving forces by these two criteria. The object is to identify the two or three that are most important and most uncertain.
- *Choose how many scenarios to develop.* It is best to have either two or four. Two is better as the difference between them is clear.

Having three can be dangerous, as many people have a tendency to go for the middle scenario for no better reason than it appears to be the moderate option or the halfway house.

- *Flesh out the scenarios.* Turn the factors into a plausible narrative. Make the title of each scenario as dramatic as possible.
- *Select leading indicators and signposts.* These are events or circumstances which will enable you to tell when part of a particular scenario happens in reality.
- *Dramatise the scenarios.* You can do this by devising snappy titles, making a cartoon, turning them into a story or developing a role play, which all help to make them more memorable.

Scenarios offer a focal point for discussing strategic options and how they might develop. Scenarios can also serve to heighten awareness of the strategic planning process in the organisation.

Exercise 22 Explaining scenarios

The board of trustees of your organisation has heard about scenario writing and thinks that it might be useful. You are asked to provide a short explanation. What do you say?

- You could start by saying that the simplest definition of a scenario is that it is a picture of a possible future.
- You could stress that scenarios need to be built by the people who are going to 'own' them, so that the board of trustees has a significant role.
- You might well explain that scenario writing is fun to do.
- You could explain the process of scenario writing as outlined above, possibly giving an illustration of one you have prepared yourself or as a planning team.

Futures wheel

The futures wheel is an extra technique that can be used to explore how a strategic issue might develop. A selected issue is placed at the centre of a large sheet of paper and its implications are brainstormed until the group runs out of ideas. Potential developments are written round the issue like the spokes of a wheel. The picture of opportunities and threats which emerges can then be written up more fully. Be aware that you need to weigh the cost and risks of the negative consequences that could flow from each alternative as well as its positive effects.

Exercise 23 Framing the issues

When you have done one or more of the exercises in this section, you will have come up with a list of strategic issues facing your organisation. This exercise will help you to bring them into some sort of order.

Summarise your strategic issues and their implications by answering the following questions (you may already have some of the answers).

1   What are the issues, conflicts or dilemmas facing your organisation?
2   Why do you describe them as issues?
3   How do the issues relate to your mission and your strengths, weaknesses, opportunities and threats?
4   How will the issues affect the performance of your organisation?
5   Why are the issues important and to whom?
6   Which issues can you do something about?
7   What would be the consequences of not doing anything about the issues?
8   Can some of the issues be combined or eliminated?
9   Will consolidating the issues into two or more major issues make your options clearer?

10 Have you omitted any issues?

11 Will tackling the issues require the allocation of any organisational resources? If so, what will this involve?

12 Which are the critical issues for the future?

Especially if you have a large number of issues facing you, it is essential to establish which have the highest priority. For example, one US city managed to identify 157 issues, which is an impossible number to deal with all at once.

Exercise 24 Setting priorities

This exercise is best carried out by the planning team as a whole so that everyone can contribute their views.

Your task is to prioritise the issues you have identified by rating three factors – probability, impact and maturity – on a scale of 1 to 5.

- To assess probability, consider the question, 'What is the likelihood that this will develop into a major issue?'
- To assess impact, consider the question, 'If this becomes a major issue, how great would its impact be on the organisation?'
- To assess maturity, consider the question, 'When will this issue become a major issue?'

Strategic issues where maturity is a factor can be divided into three groups:

- those that require no action at present but which must be monitored;
- those that require urgent attention and which must be dealt with, if necessary out of sequence with the regular strategic planning timetable;
- those that can be handled as part of the organisation's regular strategic planning activities.

Once you have rated each issue, allocate relative weights to the importance of probability, impact and maturity to your organisation's circumstances out of a total of 100 per cent (for example, you could allocate 40 per cent to probability and 30 per cent to impact and to maturity if you consider that the likelihood of a particular issue happening is more important to be aware of than its possible impact or timing). The maturity factor can be further broken down by allocating differential weights to each of the three subgroups described above, for example out of a total of 30 per cent, 15 per cent to issues requiring urgent attention and 7.5 per cent to each of the other two groups.

The calculation to work out the final ratings for each issue would then be as follows:

(Rating from 1 to 5 for probability) x (percentage for probability) = (relative weight for probability)

(Rating from 1 to 5 for impact) x (percentage for impact) = (relative weight for impact)

(Rating from 1 to 5 for maturity) x (percentage for maturity) = (relative weight for maturity)

Add together the relative weights to give you the final rating for each issue.

For example, you may have chosen three strategic issues, A, B and C.

- You consider that issue A is very likely to become important, so you give it a probability rating of 5. However, it would not have a very great impact, so you give it an impact rating of 2. It is likely to become important within the next year, so you give it a maturity rating of 4.
- Issue B you give ratings of 4, 3 and 4; issue C 1, 5 and 5. You will notice that each of these ratings adds up to 11.
- You consider that it is relatively more important for your organisation to be aware of those issues which are likely to

have the greatest impact rather than to estimate when they will take place. Therefore you have allocated relative weights of 30% to probability, 40% to impact and 30% to maturity.

- You calculate the final rating for each issue as follows:

$$A - \quad 5 \times 30\% = 1.5$$
$$2 \times 40\% = 0.8$$
$$4 \times 30\% = 1.2$$
$$1.5 + 0.8 + 1.2 = 3.5$$

$$B - \quad 4 \times 30\% = 1.2$$
$$3 \times 40\% = 1.2$$
$$4 \times 30\% = 1.2$$
$$1.2 + 1.2 + 1.2 = 3.6$$

$$C - \quad 1 \times 30\% = 0.3$$
$$5 \times 40\% = 2.0$$
$$5 \times 30\% = 1.5$$
$$0.3 + 2.0 + 1.5 = 3.8$$

So while the initial ratings you gave to the three issues seemed to be identical, ie 11, the relative weightings are different and C has the highest priority.

Example – a set of strategic issues

Greenwich Educational Psychology Service cast its strategic issues in the form of questions, as follows:

- How does the Service develop greater quality and consistency in its service to schools?
- How does the Service meet the range of statutory requirements introduced by the 1988 Education Reform Act?
- How does the Service expand user perception of the range of work it could offer and influence their priorities on the use and purchase of Service time?

- How does the Service contribute most effectively to the evolution of Education Authority policies?
- How does the Service address effectively issues of equality of opportunity?
- How does the Service maintain sufficient resourcing to be effective?
- How does the Service respond most effectively to national concerns and legislation on child protection and children in need?
- How does the Service respond positively to rapid external change?

The value chain

Strategic options can also be generated by means of a value chain. The consumer/user value chain (called 'the chain' from now on) starts by building a picture of the organisation. The chain is the sequence of processes that provides value to the consumer or user. For example, the first process might be identifying needs, while the last might be reviewing the quality of service delivery.

The advantages of the chain approach are that:

- It directs attention to the end user for whom the organisation exists.
- It provides a systematic basis for analysing all the activities which an organisation performs.
- It provides a holistic approach for the organisation which prompts you to look at the interrelationship between different activities.
- It can be used to examine the boundaries between activities, which is often where the problems arise.
- For organisations that are competing directly with others, it is a means of understanding which parts of the organisation are competitive and which are not.

- The chain is even useful in small voluntary organisations which have several distinct processes in the delivery of their service.
- It can be applied to voluntary organisations with many different concerns.

The value chain is most useful for service providers which have clearly defined users and are likely to be in direct competition with others. Other voluntary organisations – campaigning, self-help and intermediary – are likely to prefer the issues approach. They will find it harder to identify users and are likely to have external stakeholders other than users to whom they need to pay attention.

This section explains how to assemble a value chain for a voluntary organisation. To assemble its chain, the organisation groups together the key processes involved in delivering its service in sequence. The chain also includes the factors making up the infrastructure of the organisation – the personnel function, the financial management, the information systems and so on. The chain allows you to assess their contribution to the value and effectiveness of the organisation.

To construct the chain you allocate different weights to different parts of the operation in relation to how they contribute to achieving the organisation's goals. You represent this on paper by the different space you give to the different parts in the chain. This allows you to show, for example, whether carrying out the activities themselves adds more value than promoting or marketing the organisation. The weights you allocate will vary with your organisation's culture, structure and environment.

It is possible for a voluntary organisation to have several different chains. A national voluntary organisation might have one overall chain. It could also have a series of subsidiary and differently weighted chains for rural areas, or for those areas with a strong multilingual or multicultural aspect.

A chain for a voluntary organisation might look like the one in Figure 6.

Figure 6 A Value Chain

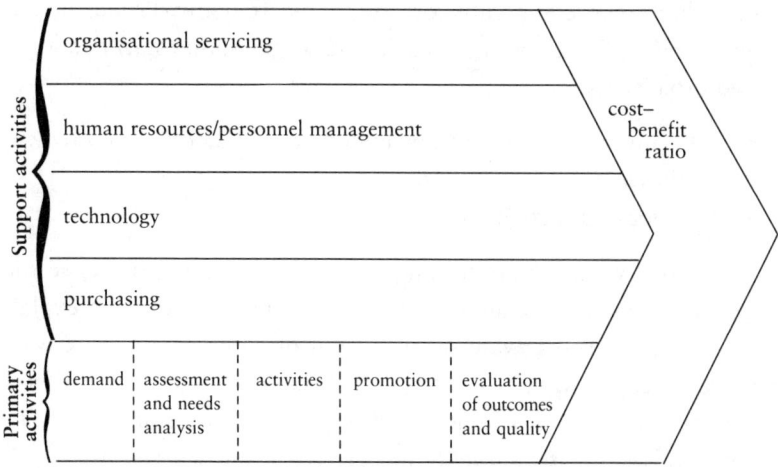

The chain can also be used to explain where value is being added for internal users and customers in the organisation. This would apply, for example, if you were delivering a service to the part of the organisation responsible for promotion. Internal customers will have views about the different parts of the service.

Exercise 25 Value chain

- Working in a group, draw a value chain for your organisation.
- Analyse the chain by answering the following questions:
  - Which parts add value?
  - How much value?
  - At what cost?
  - What quantitative benefits are there?
  - What qualitative benefits are there?
  - Are there current operations that are overvalued?
  - Are there current operations that are undervalued?

Throughout this book, we have stressed the importance of finding out what other, comparable organisations are doing. Producing and analysing a value chain should help your organisation start to address two broader issues:

- Does any other organisation undertake this activity? If so, why should we?
- How does our activity add value?

When the value chain technique is used in the private sector, organisations are encouraged to identify the factors which explain their success. The private sector notion of value is connected with profit. In contrast, the voluntary sector chain explains the creation of whatever it is the users value. An example could be a standard of care which raises the user's level of independence and self-reliance.

Strategic issues tend to look at parts of the organisation's work in isolation. This is an essential starting point, but it should not be the finishing point. Having divided the whole into pieces, it is important to put it back together again. The advantage this time is that you can use the additional knowledge and information that you have about the different parts.

Identifying the processes you carry out and the value each adds helps you work out what you are good at. From this, you can work out what you do better than other people or can learn to do better than other people. Sometimes this involves separate parts of the organisation; but often it involves the different parts of the organisation working together.

Return to SWOT

If you find it difficult to establish the relative values of the different parts of your value chain, a more sophisticated SWOT analysis might help. SWOT analysis is also useful for analysing issues.

You will remember the SWOT analysis from Chapter 3. One thing it is important to stress is that you must be honest about your organisation's weaknesses. Not being open about them does not mean that others do not see them or know about them. It is unwise to assume that others know as little about you as you may know about them. Indeed, they may have knowledge or insights about your organisation that you do not have yourself.

One weakness of SWOT analyses is that they can lead to long lists of factors which are then not correlated. There is often an over-concentration on opportunities and strengths and insufficient consideration of the obstacles posed by weaknesses and threats. The following two exercises will help you to overcome this problem.

Exercise 26 Advanced SWOT

This is a group exercise. It takes one stage further the factors you identified from the SWOT analysis you conducted in Chapter 3.

Redistribute your strengths, weaknesses, opportunities and threats as shown in the diagram below. In other words, identify the strengths which relate to opportunities, the strengths which relate to threats, and so on.

	Strengths	Weaknesses
Opportunities		
Threats		

Discuss answers to the following questions:

- How are the strengths going to be sustained by the opportunities?
- How are the weaknesses going to be lessened, particularly where they combine with threats?
- What significance do these interrelationships have for the current position and development of the organisation?
- What impact are these interrelationships likely to have on the process of formulating strategy?
- Has identification of the interrelationships shown you any additional strategic issues of which you had previously not been aware?

Exercise 27   Analysing interrelationships

This is a group exercise.

1 Identify which of the interrelationships you established in Exercise 26 are pulling your organisation away from its vision.

2 Identify which of the interrelationships are pulling your organisation towards its vision.

3 Take the most important strategic issues from those you prioritised in Exercise 24.   Review the impact of the interrelationships on each of these issues.

4 Ask the group to suggest actions which could be taken to deal with the impact of the interrelationships, that is, to build on strengths, overcome weaknesses, exploit opportunities and head off threats.

5 Review the feasibility of each suggestion in the light of the likely response of stakeholders and the available resources.

It is valuable to try to do an analysis of your organisation's strengths and weaknesses as seen by users. How can you find about what users think? Perhaps you have done a recent user survey which offers some information you can use. It may tell you about the image of the organisation, how friendly the service is, how good those services are in the eyes of the users. Maybe you could find a college student to help carry out a user survey for you if you have not already done one. Alternatively, you might want to commit yourself to some 'naive listening' to users, first ridding yourself of any preconceived notions about what they might say. This can be a very effective way to learn about their real feelings and ideas.

A further way in which SWOT can be used is to compare your organisation with your competitors and collaborators.

Exercise 28   SWOT of competitors and collaborators

1 Carry out a quick SWOT analysis of each of your competitors and collaborators, focusing mainly on strengths and weaknesses.

2 Compare your organisation's strengths and weaknesses with those identified for your competitors and collaborators. If you find that one of your strengths is shared by another organisation, delete it from your list, until you are left with just your distinctive strengths. If you are unlucky enough to find that all your strengths are deleted, don't panic! Track back and find distinctive *combinations* of strengths instead.

It can be beneficial to repeat this exercise later as you get to know more about your competitors and collaborators.

Dealing with strengths and weaknesses

The various SWOT analyses which you have conducted will have provided a vast amount of information. In the same way that you had to prioritise the strategic issues, you need to carry out a similar exercise for the results of the SWOT analyses. Different exercises may produce different sets of priorities, depending on their focus.

Now that you have the information, what are you going to do with it? One of the most important things to do is to identify how to neutralise weaknesses and make them strengths, and how to turn strengths into opportunities.

Strengths which cannot fuel opportunities have little value. If there are major opportunities in areas where your organisation is not particularly strong, you need to plan to develop your capabilities in that area.

Avoid the easy answer – 'if only we had £10,000 more', and so on. There is also a temptation to frame problems so that their root is external, seeing the organisation as a victim. Instead, problems need to be expressed so that your organisation can see what it can control. For example, the problem might appear to you to be that an external force, say the maintenance department, does not maintain the machinery well enough. The actual problem might be that you have not found the right way to communicate to that department your need for the machinery to be up to a particular standard.

Exercise 29 Dealing with strengths and weaknesses

This is a group exercise. Before the meeting distribute copies of the results of the SWOT analysis focusing on how you are seen by users, and of your distinctive strengths resulting from the comparison with competitors and collaborators.

1 Discuss ways in which the weaknesses could first be neutralised, and then be turned into strengths.

2 Explore how the strengths perceived by users can be turned into opportunities.

3 Rate opportunities and threats as high, medium or low according to their impact and probability.

Relating SWOT to the value chain

Conclusions derived from the various SWOT analyses should now enable you to assess the relative weights of the different parts of your value chain. In making your assessment, look particularly at those processes in your organisation where opportunities can build on strengths and where threats could allow present weaknesses to become entrenched.

You might decide, for example, to give more attention to promoting the organisation, an area of weakness that should not be allowed to deteriorate. Alternatively, you might decide that some activities that were previously done externally could be more successfully done internally.

SWOT analyses can be carried out for individual processes to establish the elements which are adding value. For example, the World Wide Fund for Nature selected nine key areas of its operation and did a SWOT analysis for each of them.

Cost–benefit matrix

A cost–benefit matrix is a useful tool to help you produce or revise a value chain. The matrix outlines the positive effects of particular strategies and the relative costs of pursuing them. It involves you in identifying the 'opportunity costs' of specific actions, the cost of the investment of resources or time involved in terms of its best alternative use. It also sets a framework for the consideration of non-monetary benefits and costs. It requires you to assess the uncertainties involved.

Cost–benefit analysis is not simply a way of measuring where you are but also of working on how to improve it. To create a specific cost–benefit matrix you rank costs and their respective benefits, whether they relate to activities or promotion or other parts of the chain. While cost may be easily established, it is harder to quantify benefits. One reason for this is that different stakeholders will have different views of the worth of the benefits. They will probably also have differing degrees of influence to impose their viewpoint. Asking users and internal customers is nevertheless a help to you in reaching your own conclusions.

Exercise 30 Cost–benefit matrix

1 Draw a cost–benefit matrix for your organisation by placing your activities and services on the matrix below.

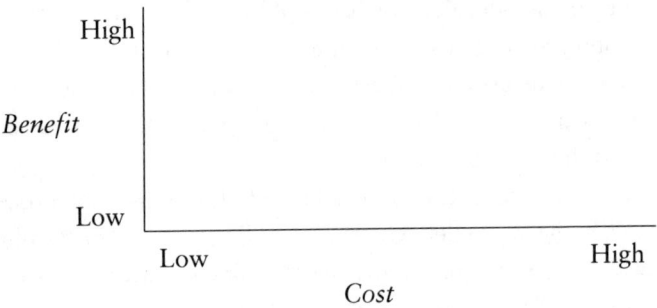

2 Compare the cost–benefit matrix with the portfolio analysis you conducted in Exercise 10.

3 Complete the value chain for your organisation.

4 Consider ways of improving the cost–benefit relationship. Suitable steps might include:

- eliminating activities that are low benefit and high cost
- greater efficiency to obtain greater benefit for the same cost
- reducing service levels to reduce cost by reducing the benefit
- changes in the way the service is organised

5 Individually or in a group draw up a full list of strategic issues for your organisation that the value chain analysis and cost–benefit relationship raise.

Critical success factors (CSFs)

This section brings together the two separate routes to generating strategic options outlined in this chapter – the issues approach and the value chain. If people in an organisation are asked what has made that organisation successful or unsuccessful they may come up with a long list of reasons. It could be the image and history of the organisation, or the personality of the organisation's chair, the weakness of those competing for resources, the assets the organisation holds and so on.

Critical success factors are what they say they are. They are the factors critical for the success of the organisation. They are the things that must be done well. For those facing market challenges, they are the limited number of areas in which satisfactory results will ensure competitive performance. Both critical success factors and SWOT analysis are ways of identifying the factors which contribute most to your success. SWOT analysis offers a speedy route to their identification, but CSFs allow greater precision.

The success of this stage of the process rests on thorough preparation so that uncertainty has been reduced to the point where you can make a judgement. CSFs may provide answers to many of the questions thrown up by the process of identifying strategic issues.

You may be wondering what the difference is between strategic issues and CSFs. Strategic issues are the key questions, whereas critical success factors provide some or all of the answers. For example, a strategic issue for a voluntary organisation might be 'we don't receive many legacies'. As a CSF, this might be expressed as 'we could attract more legacies by preparing a guide to writing a will'. Even if this was only expressed as 'we must attract more legacies', this would at least imply that the organisation had decided to try to obtain them as opposed to looking elsewhere for funds.

The number of CSFs that an organisation produces for itself is a sign of its cohesion. One study asked managers in each of 125 European companies to list CSFs for their company. The number of CSFs listed was between 6 and 12 for the 40 most profitable companies and between 26 and 43 for the 40 least profitable. It is interesting to note that one company in the latter group was prompted to agree on fewer, more defined objectives and later moved into the more profitable set. We recommend that the maximum number of CSFs is 8 to 14 if the organisation's survival is at stake. Some writers say 8 is the magic number, but this is too rigid. If you produce too many, it may simply be that they are defined at too great a level of detail.

Exercise 31   Generating CSFs

This is a group exercise. Allow plenty of time – between 1 and 3 hours. You could undertake the exercise by considering the whole organisation, or for one function, or even for an individual manager, staff member or volunteer.

1   Start with a 10-minute brainstorming session (see Appendix 1). Ask the group to provide single words which indicate factors which could help your organisation achieve its mission.

2   Reframe these words into phrases beginning 'We need' or 'We must'. The use of 'we' makes it a collective choice, while the 'need' or 'must' emphasises its importance. These are your critical success factors.

3   Each CSF must cover one issue only, and must be necessary to achieve the mission. Together they should be sufficient to achieve it.

4   You are likely to produce a mixture of strategic and tactical CSFs. For example, a strategic CSF might be 'We must successfully manage the transition from the National Association of Development Education Centres to the Development Education Association', a tactical CSF 'We must get our newsletters out on time'. Concentrate on the strategic CSFs.

5 Rank the CSFs according to their significance for the organisation, taking into account possible expansion, desired image, services provided, calibre of management and so on. Consider whether over time each CSF might become more or less significant for the organisation.

6 Review the interaction between the factors – what significant combinations emerge?

Exercise 32 Linking CSFs to options

1 Develop a matrix of CSFs and processes by placing processes along the top and critical success factors down the side (see example below).

Processes

	Needs analysis	Assessment	Activities	Evaluation
Membership				
Quality of service				
CSFs User involvement				
Fundraising				
Image				

2 Rank the processes according to the number of CSFs they help to achieve.

In our experience critical success factors are likely to lie in the following areas:

- *control of resources* – with the focus on planning and rational decision making in budgeting and monitoring;
- *culture* – with the focus on organisational and staff development;
- *dealing with future uncertainties;*
- *power* – with the focus on understanding and influencing stakeholders and outside interest groups.

Once you have established your CSFs, someone within the organisation needs to take responsibility for each one. His or her role should be to see that the CSFs are monitored and that performance on each one is used to motivate staff, volunteers, and the board of trustees.

You may want to return to your list of CSFs after your strategic options have been chosen to see whether you have gained any further insights into what makes your organisation successful.

Preparing to plan your strategic action

The final sections of this chapter provide a bridge to action planning. They develop options for tackling issues that you identified earlier. This section and the next are likely to be most useful to service providers.

One way of approaching action planning is to consider what strategy will give the organisation unique sustained advantage. The use of the term 'advantage' is deliberate. We are assuming that many voluntary organisations will find themselves in a more competitive arena than they are used to. The idea of advantage draws on the distinctive strengths of your organisation identified earlier in this chapter. Such sustained advantage tends to be around:

- competitive cost and price of a specific service
- overall cost control in the organisation
- quality of service
- capacity for innovation
- the ability to hold onto a specific service or campaigning niche.

Identification of your source of advantage may have to be counter-balanced by political demands made on you by the external environment or your stakeholders.

Developing strategic options

Having identified the strategic issues facing your organisation, you now need to decide how to tackle them. Strategic options can be developed using the technique of goal wishing, which emphasises the organisation's ambitions. It is designed to list barriers to thinking more laterally.

Exercise 33 Goal wishing

This is a group exercise. Distribute copies of the list of strategic issues and the results of the value chain analysis.

1 Using brainstorming (see Appendix 1) devise as many ways as possible for the organisation to deal with each issue. These are your strategic options.

2 Explore the advantages and disadvantages of each approach suggested. Keep a note of the discussion.

You may find it helpful to use the devil's advocate technique outlined in Appendix 1 to make sure that you view the problem from all sides.

Exercise 34 Working for sustained advantage

This is a group exercise. Distribute copies of the lists of strategic issues and critical success factors, and the strategic options resulting from Exercise 33 and the results of the value chain analysis.

Aim to answer the following questions. Some may require research to be carried out, so you will need to arrange for a follow-up meeting.

1 Which are the most feasible strategic options for our organisation to pursue?

2 What are the barriers to following each of these alternative routes? Who is competing or collaborating with us?

3 How can these barriers be overcome now and in the immediate future?

4 What must staff, volunteers and the board of trustees do to make these options a reality?

5 What actions should be taken in the immediate future to start implementing these proposals? Are any of these actions in conflict with each other, and what can we do about that?

Having answered the questions in Exercise 34 you will be able to set out what the organisation is willing to commit itself to over the coming period and in the immediate future in relation to the more fundamental issues.

The strategic options that you have developed will tend to fall into one of three usually distinct groups:

- Strategies that are protective, aiming to enable the organisation to maintain its current position and minimise risk.
- Strategies that are far more innovative, carry certain risks, are difficult to imitate, and are inspired by the significant benefit they will bring to the organisation.
- Strategies that are co-operative, where the effort is put into reducing uncertainty or avoiding insularity through collaborating with other similar organisations.

We would counsel against presenting too many strategic options. This tends to make the subsequent discussions too diffuse and it can be demotivating for the people involved because of the volume of material they have to absorb. You will need to choose some criteria in order to evaluate the options. Here is a suggested list:

- fit with mission, values and vision
- timescale
- impact on users
- flexibility
- fit with 'mini strategies' being pursued by the organisation
- fit with the environment over the period covered by the strategy
- availability of resources
- fit with the culture

Rank each option against the criteria you choose. You can do this informally, by marking each option as having high, medium or low attractiveness; or you can do it more formally and score each option with between 1 and 5 for each criterion.

This is only a first attempt at deciding on your favoured strategic options. The reason for this is that we have left until the next chapter the question of capability, of whether the organisation has the capacity and the will to implement a particular option.

Action points

On the basis of the exercises and advice in this chapter, you should now be in a position to undertake four key actions:

1 Establish the strategic thinking of the leaders of your organisation.

2 Build scenarios to help you cope with future uncertainty.

3 Produce a flow chart for the stages and timing of strategy preparation in your organisation. This is a time chart which shows particular actions in the sequence in which they need to be carried out.

4 Choose your most attractive strategic options.

Chapter 6
Can You Make it Happen?

> The ultimate skill for change mastery . . . consists of the ability to conceive, construct, and convert into behavior a new view of organizational reality.
>
> *Rosabeth Moss Kanter*

This chapter helps you to assemble the power you need to make your strategy happen. It considers whether the organisation wants to make the change and whether it can. It also shows you how to finalise the strategy, turn it into a plan, and communicate it inside and outside the organisation. Strategy involves more than deciding what you need to do to achieve your mission. It involves being able to display considerable willpower in order to secure change.

Before reading further, it is important that you have worked on the exercises in Chapter 5 and explored key options for your organisation. Doing this may have given you confidence that your organisation is able to make the transition to developing and implementing new and more effective strategies. You may feel that your organisation has learnt all it needs to before plunging into the implementation phase.

This chapter encourages you to pause. Key questions to ask now are:

- Do people involved in or with the organisation, including staff, members and trustees, want to make the changes you plan?
- Is the organisation really capable of making those changes?

Organisational capability

Capability means your ability to make things happen. Organisational capability depends on the ability of the organisation to learn from its internal and external environment, and for all those involved in the organisation to participate in this learning process. An organisation that cannot learn, like the foreman who went on the interpersonal skills course we mentioned in Chapter 3, will never be able to implement a strategy successfully because it will always be trying to do new things in the old way.

The focus of Chapter 5 was on establishing the capacity of your organisation to fit strategy to purpose. The ability to learn extends the capacity of the organisation to respond to difficult circumstances and to change. Learning and the will to change tend to stimulate each other. Once the ability to learn is established, finding the resources required for change can be tackled with much greater confidence.

Learning is used here to mean work or organisation based learning rather than any kind of external study. We are concerned with both self-managed and organisation-led learning.

Testing your organisation's ability to learn

There are five useful tests of an organisation's learning ability:

- How much has the organisation already learnt about its problems and the range of possible solutions?
- Have novel solutions been found?
- Is the organisation encouraging the individual learning and personal development of its staff and volunteers?
- How much is two-way communication in the organisation used to support learning and development?
- How far is the organisation able to involve its users and the wider public as part of the process of challenging the way things are done?

An organisation's ability to learn is fundamentally affected by its culture and style. Some further questions to ask to explore the relationship are:

- Will the chosen strategic options conflict with the organisation's usual style of operating?
- What aspects of the organisation's deliberate and emergent strategies could support and encourage a commitment to organisational learning?
- Is your organisation locked into a pattern of behaviour or assumptions that place a block on its learning?
- Does it have certain mindsets (fixed mental attitudes) or a tendency for 'groupthink' that will obstruct its intended strategy?
- Is the organisation prepared to support project based and action learning in groups and teams? (In action learning groups learn through working on work problems that the members are currently facing.)

If you are not satisfied with the answers to these questions, you could plot what you see as your organisation's limitations in what Johnson and Scholes call a 'cultural web'. At the heart of the cultural web is a model of the organisation which characterises the way in which the organisation sees the outside world. This is called a paradigm, and it is intended to capture the core of an organisation's culture. The paradigm is shaped by:

- the routine ways members of the organisation behave towards each other;
- the rituals of organisational life, such as career progression;
- the stories told by members of the organisation;
- the more symbolic aspects of the organisation, eg its logos;
- the control systems, eg performance indicators;
- the power structures;
- the formal organisational structure and the more informal ways that the organisation works.

Exercise 35 Finding your organisation's paradigm

1 Work out what your organisation's paradigm – characteristic model – is now. To do this, place a circle entitled 'our organisation' in the centre of a piece of flipchart paper. Position seven circles around it entitled 'routine', 'rituals', 'stories', 'symbols', 'control systems', 'power structures' and 'organisational structure'. As a group, brainstorm points which set the boundaries for your organisation's approach to making change. Allocate each point to the appropriate circle when you have reached agreement.

2 What would you want the new paradigm to be to ensure that your strategy can be implemented and sustained?

3 What shortcomings have you identified in your organisation? How are you going to address them? What does this tell you about how your organisation will behave in the face of the changes indicated by the strategy?

When doing this exercise, you may find it helpful to refer back to the exercises on purpose, mission and vision in Chapter 4.

Dealing with obstructions to organisational learning

It would be very surprising if you did not discover ways in which your organisation obstructed learning. Peter Senge, a US management thinker, identifies five useful principles to deal with such obstructions.

Encourage personal mastery

Individual learning and personal development clarify and deepen our personal vision and are more likely to support organisational vision and mission. For example, the Women's Environmental Network sends its staff and volunteers on training courses in assertiveness and self-esteem. What scope does your organisation provide for personal growth?

Explore mental models

Mental models are our hidden assumptions, mindsets or prejudices about the way the world works. They could take the form of generalisations, pictures, images or stories. We have no hope of developing new mental models until we bring our hidden assumptions out into the open.

Build a shared vision

A shared picture of a desired future creates enormous energy. However, you cannot force people to sign up to a vision. The process of creating it has to be genuinely participative (as described in Chapter 4). Too often the head of an organisation talks about 'our vision' when she or he really means 'my vision'.

Commit to team learning

Teams are crucial to how an organisation learns. Effective group work, in particular the ability to build positively on ideas rather than encourage competitive group practices, is vital in developing an organisational strategy that is able to be implemented.

Develop systems thinking

Look for interrelationships between the parts and the whole. This builds on the value chain activities in Chapter 5.

Key steps in building your organisation's capability

Senge's five principles underline how essential it is for voluntary organisations to devise ways of drawing fully on sources of strength when embarking on major change. There are four building blocks that help to overcome blockages and develop capabilities.

Utilise the skills and knowledge of the staff and volunteers

Training both on and off the job is important in developing skills and knowledge, tapping underutilised potential and overcoming frustrations. More than this, the empowerment of staff through delegation and involvement in decision-making processes will enhance their contribution to strategy.

The assumption is often made that strategy is not for first line managers. For instance, the Management Charter Initiative Level 1 (National Vocational Qualification Level 4) does not include assessment of any competence in strategy. We have given many reasons in this book why such people should be involved in strategy making.

Exercise 36   A presentation about implementation

This exercise is intended to help you focus your ideas about how you are going to implement your strategy.

Imagine that you are going to give a presentation to your staff and volunteers about your strategic options and how you are going to implement them. You want to engage their interest and involvement in the implementation process.

Prepare the text for a maximum of six OHP slides for this presentation, with no more than six lines to each slide and six words on each line.

Develop good systems and structures

Systems and structures are always important. How is your organisation designed to carry out its strategic purposes? The existing systems and structure of your organisation will reflect past learning within the organisation and influence current learning. Often the rules and procedures reflect the past. They may be obsessed with detail to the point of obscuring the purpose of the organisation. Equally, systems might not be able to pull together data from different sources that would help to examine how the organisation might shift position, change direction, adapt to new circumstances and so on.

Systems and structures can help the organisation change. For example, over the last few years flatter structures have been devised to enable organisations to adopt a more flexible and responsive approach.

However before rushing to change systems and structures it is important to consider the best timing for the move. For example, the Youth Hostel Association decided to change its structure first. It had to ensure that the development of its strategy was sufficiently far advanced so that the organisation did not end up with a structure that proved contradictory to the final strategy. Structural change is often costly and painful. You want to get it right and don't want to have to do it too often. Structural change can be phased in, but the difficulties involved may quite reasonably lead you to tackling it as the last part of your strategy.

Change the culture

In Chapter 3 we stressed the importance of an organisation's culture in shaping the strategy it might pursue. All the 'rational' planning arguments in the world will not of themselves achieve a good strategy if the culture of the organisation rules it out. Cultures are not static, although change in them often comes about slowly. On the other hand, they can be very difficult to change and can sometimes change in unexpected directions, so if you choose this approach be very sure of what you want to achieve.

Develop strategic alliances

One way of overcoming internal obstacles is to develop strategic alliances, collaborative ventures with other organisations. Strategic alliances can play an important part in changing and developing an organisation's practices. Whether they concern service delivery, fundraising or campaigning, they can help your organisation to secure capabilities that it does not possess on its own. They can develop the organisation's capability and make the best use of its resources. While all organisations should be selective about the alliances they enter into, your desire to set up alliances may not fit with your organisation's culture. Some organisations have an approach to their work which dampens any enthusiasm for alliances.

Encountering resistance

There is likely to be resistance to strategic change in some parts of your organisation. By resistance we mean any behaviour that tries to maintain the status quo in the face of pressure to change it. It may be that those resisting have their own strategy. The resistance can be cultural, social, organisational or psychological. It is important to explore its sources, intensity and focus.

Exercise 37 Visualising obstacles to change

For this exercise you need to have defined a major change facing your organisation and the key objectives of that change.

1 Visualise your organisation's environment as a series of cross-country motorcycle tracks (or rally or orienteering course if you prefer). Draw the outline of the tracks on a very large piece of paper. Mark the starting line and the finishing line. In order to achieve the desired change your organisation needs to cover the track from beginning to end.

2 Identify the formal, overt barriers or obstacles to your organisation achieving the change (eg poor strategy, policy, undesirable behaviour, obstructive procedures). Draw these as rough or waterlogged sections of track. The more important they are, the larger the amount of track they cover.

3 Identify the informal obstacles (culture, values, attitudes) and draw them as the rest of the course, showing the fixed assumptions you must respect.

4 Can you find different, more effective ways round the barriers to reach your objective?

5 As you go forward what do you see in front of you? How does the picture change?

6 Will one circuit of the course be enough to work through the problems? Remember that strategy is an iterative process, one that repeats itself.

Dealing effectively with resistance can be a complex task and requires thorough preparation. You need to think about how you can weaken the link between change and the negative consequences that people are afraid of.

Exercise 38 Spotting resistance

Think about changes which your organisation has gone through in the past. List the ways that resistance to change revealed themselves.

Examples could include various 'games' that may be played, notably around budget time (x has to take priority, savings should never be made on y); frustration frequently evident in staff meetings; the part trade unions are often pressed to play in organisations.

In Chapter 3 we considered briefly the relationship between strategy making and conflict. Conflict is likely to have its roots in one of three different sources:

- *different methods* being used to achieve common goals – the conflict might well be procedural;
- *inconsistent goals* – people in one part of the organisation choose a course of action which is incompatible with another of the organisation's goals. Lack of clear goals is included in inconsistent goals. Has your strategy process resolved the inconsistent goals?

- *resources* – goals of different parts of the organisation often raise conflicting demands on resources.

Before you can deal with resistance or conflict you have to understand it fully. Answering the following questions might help:

- Is there a personal vendetta masquerading as procedural issues?
- What is the strength as well as the weakness of your opponents' arguments? Perhaps they are right and part of the strategy should be revised, or at least reviewed. Your version of reality might not be the only one. The resistance could be playing a positive role by challenging assumptions that need to be questioned.
- Is the information on which you base your analysis open to a different interpretation? Those modernising the Youth Hostel Association could initially point to good results. After the recession hit, the opponents of the change argued that the results were cyclical.
- Is the change not yet fully understood? If so, are the objections those commonly found at this point; for example, denying the need for change or being defensive? If so, is there reason to believe that this mood will eventually shift to adaptation, acceptance and commitment to the change?

Choice of tactics

If you need to tackle conflict, there are four elements in the situation you can try to change. You could:

- change the context, for example by reducing dependence on statutory funding;
- change the issue or task in dispute, for example by widening the team's brief;
- change the relationship between the parties in conflict, for example by spending some time on team building;
- change the people involved, for example by persuading some people to leave the team.

The tactics you choose must be those that are best suited to the objectives you want to achieve. They must also fit with the values of the organisation – is manipulation an acceptable practice in your organisation, for example?

Overcoming resistance may require compromise on your part. Making compromises is an acceptable part of strategic planning. There does, however, need to be an agreement on the fundamentals, such as the values and the mission. Not all views can be wholly accommodated in a focused mission or tight list of core values.

You also have to consider whether you need to proceed through negotiation or consultation and the time pressures that this requirement places on you. The culture of the voluntary sector values people. It is therefore especially important to reflect on how to deal with individuals' resistance to change. You might find it useful to apply one of the following recommendations for overcoming individuals' resistance to the planning process: giving the person an important assignment within the strategy-making process; talking to them individually about the value of their contribution; soliciting their comments in meetings; and enlisting the support of respected colleagues in persuading them to your view.

In general, resolving conflict calls for a degree of understanding and skill. You will need to start by acknowledging that the conflict exists. The issue or problem should be clearly defined. A search should be initiated for alternative solutions, if there are any, and these should then be evaluated in order to try to reach an agreement.

In summary, you will need to establish the best ways to 'unfreeze' the present position. Unfreezing involves getting people to accept that there is a need for change. You can then begin to institute change before 'refreezing' the organisation in the desired new position.

Resistance from stakeholders

The focus of the previous section has been on dealing with internal resistance. It is also very important to assess the views of any potentially antagonistic external stakeholders. You can do this by:

- identifying the stakeholders who are relevant;
- looking for potential coalitions by identifying neutral and less important stakeholders who may be working with antagonistic stakeholders;
- taking steps to block the formation of coalitions among antagonistic and neutral stakeholders;
- preventing antagonistic stakeholders from undermining supporters;
- determining which antagonistic stakeholders must be surprised in order to delay or prevent them mobilising their opposition – think carefully about whether this is feasible, since the tactic can backfire on you;
- anticipating the nature of opposition and developing counter arguments in advance;
- negotiating with selected antagonists to determine and perhaps adopt changes in the proposed course of action that would change them into neutrals and/or even supporters;
- giving the antagonistic stakeholders a role.

Take the initiative and use your supporters, both internal and external, to:

- provide information to reinforce positive attitudes;
- help analyse how you can build consensus between policy makers and those responsible for implementation;
- involve key supporters in some or all of the team's deliberations – build up a club atmosphere;
- ask supportive stakeholders to sell the strategy to those who are neutral.

Are there other ways you can think of to turn neutral stakeholders into supporters? Make a note of them now.

Presenting the strategy to those outside the organisation may well require a different approach to the one you adopted for people inside the organisation. As a general rule, your presentation should be short, pithy and avoid making promises or predictions you will be unable to adhere to.

Leading the change

Successful strategic change requires leadership. It is easy to pay lip-service to the importance of leadership and much harder to deliver it. What will cause leaders and leadership to be accepted? One way of putting it is that in order to gain Acceptance leaders need:

- Belief
- Clarity
- Determination
- Empathy

Symbolic acts are often powerful. One US chief executive decided to stop tasting the sausages his company produced. He did this to give his workers the powerful message that he was entrusting them with the quality of the company's sausages.

Achieving a core of support for strategic change among the leadership group is a vital element in successful leadership. Staff changes for whatever reason can make this process easier as the new postholders are less tied to past practice. In the case of the Abbeyfield Society, for example, the chief executive's review has been aided by the fact that three out of five departmental heads are new and one has been in post only 15 months.

Lasting change means that the people involved change. Leaders can create the conditions for change. In the words of ICL, the computer company, 'People change, but we don't change people'. One of the infinite number of lightbulb jokes is, 'How may psychotherapists does it take to change a lightbulb?' Answer: 'Only one, but the lightbulb has to want to change.'

So leaders need to leave space for people to learn, make mistakes and change. There is a saying, 'The captain bites his tongue until it bleeds'. This refers to a superior watching a junior officer bringing a big ship into harbour for the first time. The director of the Women's Environmental Network has a sign above her desk which is her response to colleagues seeking reassurance, 'Use your own best judgement at all times'.

Exercise 39 Assessing freedom to make mistakes

How much freedom to make mistakes do staff and volunteers have in your organisation?

If you are a manager, list three recent examples when you have allowed staff or volunteers to make mistakes.

I What was your response to the mistakes? Did you:

- take back the responsibility
- give those involved more responsibilities
- simply solve the particular problem

2 What kind of language did you use when you spoke to those involved? Was it:

- mainly critical – 'this must never happen again'
- mainly educative – 'what can we learn from what has happened?'

There are no universal right answers to these questions. Compare your answers to the discussion of organisational capability and learning earlier in this chapter.

The organisation's leaders have to explain and keep on explaining what the strategy is all about. This will involve communication both up and down and across the organisation. It should also cover the procedures for modifying the strategy should that be needed. Any written communication should be brief (ie no more than two pages) and free from jargon.

Communication can be complex in national and regional membership organisations. Local groups can make the communication highly cost effective, but at the same time they may be a barrier to some communication. The Civic Trust, whose purpose is 'Caring for Places where People Live and Work', has many affiliated local amenity societies. It has found it much easier to communicate through those societies than directly to their individual members.

Improved communication has political implications in some organisations. To return to the Civic Trust, its local societies have gained representation on its Council and accumulated influence in their own right. For example, they now seek to meet Ministers themselves rather than leaving it to the Council.

Communication consists not only of words, spoken or written. It also consists of behaviour. If someone's words are in conflict with their actions, people will believe the actions. Albert Schweitzer, the missionary, said, 'There are only three ways of changing people: by example; by example; and by example.' For instance, the Spastics Society wanted to proclaim its deep concern for its client group. If it had not gone about the huge task of making its offices accessible to wheelchairs, its words would have counted for little.

Here is another example of actions speaking louder than words. The directors of a not very good US clothing company were told to order themselves some clothes, and then made to wear the results, however ill fitting, at a sales conference. No words could have achieved the same effect.

Leadership is an exhausting business. It is worth trying to retain some of your resources and energy for those times when you need to deal with unforeseen events and to help you seize unexpected opportunities.

Persuading the trustees

An important part of preparing for strategy implementation is to involve the trustees. Trustees are a much underutilised resource for planning. In organisations without staff, the trustees will have to provide the leadership referred to in the previous section. In many voluntary organisations with staff, those staff will be expected to provide some or all of the leadership for the strategic planning process.

In the Introduction, we stressed the importance of trustees being involved from the start of the process. They are the guardians of the mission and therefore must be involved in the vision. In this section, we will concentrate on ways in which trustee involvement might be secured throughout the process.

The NCVO report *On Trust* (1992) indicated that trustees are less prepared to play their traditional passive role. This does not always mean that they want to be involved with planning. Many trustees find it easier to cope with the minutiae of the organisation's existence or to focus on the immediate cause that brought them into the organisation. Achieving the trustees' involvement in the life of many voluntary organisations is a challenging process but strategic planning can be an excellent way of bringing it about.

One base line model of how to involve a board of busy trustees is called 'three bites of the cherry'. First, the general idea is introduced. No specific proposal is made but reactions are sought formally or informally. The next stage is that the framework for strategy development is presented, and approval is sought to proceed. The final stage is that a detailed draft strategy is presented for discussion at a special meeting of the trustees called solely for this purpose. The venue of the meeting may be changed to find a more relaxed environment. At the conclusion of the process, trustees are given the final document and thanked for their contribution.

In this case the board of trustees is still playing a limited role but will probably feel that its voice has been heard. The principle of 'minimum surprises' has been adhered to and the board has been given opportunities to block the process without anybody losing too much 'face'.

An approach going beyond this base line might include:

- using the specific expertise of individual trustees who have understanding or expertise in an area of strategic planning or who could facilitate the process;
- including trustees in the planning team or establishing a reference group of trustees to oversee the development of the strategy;
- providing an additional briefing session to explain the process and to allow trustees to contribute their views. This may sound passive but it gives higher status to the strategic planning process in the eyes of trustees.

There are some pitfalls to avoid when dealing with trustees. They include:

- keeping trustees ignorant of what is going on – an ignorant trustee is no asset to an organisation;
- using the wrong language in the strategy – for example, 'members' rather than 'supporters' – which may be offputting to trustees even though it has little to do with the substance of what you are saying;
- not recognising the personal interests of trustees;
- leaving out the full background to the strategy – this is particularly serious where any significant expenditure is involved;
- late briefing papers – strategy documents often have to be several pages long and may be written under pressure. All the work that is put into them may be lost if they are produced at the meeting rather than circulated in advance. Trustees may not have profound comments on what is put in front of them, but they can become very suspicious and obstructive about papers which they feel are being pushed through in an apparent hurry;
- drafts which are too glossy – they may look too polished for trustees to feel that their contribution will be taken seriously;
- patronising the board is fatal – you should pose questions to the board even if you imply the answers and this requires advance preparation;

- assuming that an approach to planning which worked with one organisation will work with another.

Martin Eede, the former chief executive of the National Schizophrenia Fellowship (NSF), contrasts his experience of planning in NSF with planning as Chief Executive of the Terrence Higgins Trust (THT). He describes the members of THT as young and energetic 'with high octane' in an organisation with strong roots in volunteering. Volunteers became involved in the planning process at a much earlier stage. In NSF the volunteers were older, more worn down by the long-term care responsibilities, and generally far less involved. Planning was a longer drawn out process.

What are the best methods of influencing and persuasion that can be applied? Our suggestions are:

- Brief the chair in advance.
- Limit the length of the plan even if it means getting a ruthless friend to edit it.
- Put it on the agenda at a point where maximum attendance can be expected to ensure the best ownership.
- Treat opponents of the strategic change seriously and with respect. In reviewing their strategy, the Youth Hostel Association made sure that the working group included representatives known to be against key proposed changes to company status. They made sure also that these were people who were respected by others against the key change.
- Avoid having a single faction which makes the decisions.
- Offer the board of trustees the opportunity of attending workshops and other training opportunities, possibly using an outside facilitator if this will make the process more comfortable. One of the workshop formats suggested in Chapter 2 could be adapted for this purpose.

In some organisations, it will be necessary to persuade a much larger group than a normal board. If you need to present to a conference or special council meeting, this will probably mean that you need to make a more formal presentation. Foster Murphy, chief executive of the Abbeyfield Society, used a 35-minute slide presentation to get over an understanding of what the outputs of the plan were, what its timescale was, and to win some understanding of the language of strategy.

Exercise 40 Rewriting a strategy document

This exercise gives you practice at writing a strategy document that is 'user friendly'.

Read the following two paragraphs which are part of a strategy document:

We believe that the curriculum framework we have developed and the teaching-learning strategies which evolve from it, embody the values of our mission. It is also a model which is designed to contribute to the college's overall strategic direction, support our main strategic priorities and facilitate the achievement of our vision. Within this context, the curriculum model has three interdependent themes:

- quality
- equality of opportunity
- entitlement

Our plan for the development of curriculum and learning strategies has been formulated in conjunction with our plans for marketing and development and finance and resources. The key implementation objectives and performance indicators which are described in the following pages are closely integrated with the corresponding strategies outlined in these plans.

Rewrite these two paragraphs in a style that would suit your trustees.

You could add to this exercise by working out what you would say in a brief presentation or speech to your trustees advocating the strategic plan. You could also look back and see how you have built on the ideas in the presentation you developed for Exercise 1.

Choosing between strategic options

You have already evaluated your strategic options against the criteria given in Chapter 5. Below is a revised list that incorporates the recommendations in this chapter so far. Evaluate the options against:

- the organisation's capability
- the desire for change, including that of the different parts of the organisation and external stakeholders
- their fit with the challenges of your environment
- their feasibility
- your organisation's capacity – the different types of resource that can be drawn on
- their appropriateness to the organisation's culture
- their appropriateness to the organisation's structure
- how well they fit the organisation's mission
- how well they fit the organisation's vision
- how well they fit the organisation's values

Example – criteria for selecting strategic options

The Smokey River First Nation, a group of Canadian Indians, used the following criteria to select its strategy from possible venture opportunities:

- organisational capacity
- employment
- interest, skills and experience
- community services/products
- start-up costs
- build on existing assets and business
- capable management
- significant training opportunities
- opportunities for shared ownership
- unique service/product

Drafting a strategy document

Strategic planning is far more than one big plan or a series of strategy documents. Plans should be written to suit their purpose, not to some abstract model of good practice. There is no blueprint, but here is some general guidance on writing a plan and other strategy documents:

- Decide early on who should write the key strategy documents.
- Keep the flipchart sheets from brainstorming and other exercises that you undertake.
- Make sure the writers have sufficient time to think about what they are writing and to pull together the document.
- Use the planning team, committees or working groups to review what has been written but not to write the plan.
- Use the chapter headings of this book to provide yourself with an initial framework and then adapt it to your needs.
- Keep the language as simple as possible.
- Keep the document as brief as is reasonable – we would recommend 5–20 pages overall with 1 or 2 pages for each section. In NADEC, a 30-page plan was thrown out because there was no ownership of it. A subsequent four-page plan was far more successful.
- If you do produce more than one plan document, remember the simple adage – too many plans spoil the broth!
- Keep in mind the different audiences for the plan – the internal audience wants a sense of direction; the external audience, notably funders, may want assurance about viability.
- Provide an executive summary for the document but write it last. This should be written so that it can be circulated widely and stand alone.

The plan or plans should be viewed as living documents open to amendment. One way of inviting updating is to place them in a looseleaf folder.

It is possible to write a plan with a very loose structure. The Whitechapel Art Gallery's 25-page three-year plan has three main parts – aims and principles, present policy and practice, and goals for the next three years. Organisations that consider this too unstructured may find the following frameworks more helpful.

Examples – strategic plans

Abbeyfield Society
The contents of the Abbeyfield Society draft strategic plan 1993–1996 are:

1 Introduction
2 Guiding Principles and Objectives
  • Principles
  • Objectives
3 Context
  • Background
  • Environment
  • A Changing Abbeyfield
4 Vision
5 Specific Strategies
  • National Committees and Regional Councils
  • Management
  • Care and Development
  • Information and Public Affairs
  • Finance and Central Services
6 Implementation
  • Timescale
  • Financial Appraisal

BTCV
The strategic plan of the British Trust for Conservation Volunteers (BTCV), covering 1993–1996, runs to 12 pages. The contents are:

1 Vision statement
2 Introduction
3 Policy Development
4 Summary
5 Direct Action by BTCV
6 Enabling others to take action
7 Support Services
8 Management
Operational plans 1993/4
Comparative Trading Statements 1987/8 to 1992/3

Some sections are subdivided. That on management, for example, covers:

- Role of Volunteers
- Developing Skills
- Quality Issues
- Equal Opportunities
- Grey Greens
- Parents with Dependent Children
- Minorities

Communicating the plan

Producing the strategic plan is an enormous labour. It is sometimes easy to forget the need to communicate it effectively. This involves choosing both the medium and the message. Particular considerations are as follows:

- Manage expectations. If you are going to conduct a consultation process on the draft plan with staff, for example, make that process clear and the decision-making process following the consultation well known. This is important in helping people to accept outcomes that they dislike.
- Use the external media and internal communications to amplify the change message. In many voluntary organisations only a

section of the membership receives a regular publication from the organisation. In the National Federation of Women's Institutes, only one-third subscribes to its magazine *Home and Country*, and only one-quarter purchases its diary.

- If communication is too routine or ritualistic, the impact is lessened.
- Make it special, not just another announcement.
- Consider the recipients' perspective. You need to have a good answer to the question 'What has this got to do with me?'
- Use face to face communication where you can.
- Take care with timing. For example, avoid shocks at Christmas and consultation in August!

Dress rehearsal

It is often possible to have a 'dress rehearsal' to test the reaction to different strategic options. This allows you to modify the strategy to take account of these reactions if necessary.

Here are some key questions to think about if you are going to have a dress rehearsal of your strategy presentation:

- Is there a way of testing the strategy? For instance, LASA had an acting director for nine months before committing itself to a permanent director.
- Is there a way of simulating the plan to test it before the resources are committed? For example, one microcomputer company simulated a plan for increased sales to find out what the assumptions were. They soon realised that 20 per cent growth in sales and in sales people implied that the productivity of the sales force would stay unchanged. There was in fact no way that new recruits could be as productive as veterans. The plan was reviewed as a consequence.
- Is there time for a trial of part of the strategy?
- Will the trial give a good picture of what the entire strategy will look like?

- Should a trial be hidden, so as not to bias the results, or open, to encourage people to own the strategy and its implementation?

Mission impossible

What do you do if you now find just before implementation that some part of the strategy is incapable of being carried out, despite having followed the approaches suggested in this chapter?

Here is a simple list of possible courses of action:

- The strategy may be overspecified. You may have been too definite about one route and have not sufficiently considered others. Is there an easier route to implementation?
- Is the language alienating people? Try to be pragmatic and change it.
- Is the amount of change too great for people to absorb now? You may need to programme some change for later rather than sooner.
- Is the pace of change too fast? Consider a shallower strategic staircase (Chapter 5), spreading the actions over a longer period or leaving the changes for a later time and invest in a change management project now, perhaps focusing on cultural change.

Action points

- Gauge your organisation's capability to carry out your strategy.
- Use capability and other criteria to select the most suitable strategic options.
- Check that the trustees are in agreement about the route you want to take.
- Write the options up into a plan.
- Have a dress rehearsal of your strategy presentation if you can.

Chapter 7
Making it Happen

My commitment is to ideas that degenerate into action. Hardly ever does this happen.

Peter Drucker

This chapter is about how you make your chosen strategy happen, about the process of implementation. The components of implementation are people, planning, measures and systems, for management information, for performance appraisal and for finance.

One of the themes of this book is that all the stages of planning are interrelated. It is especially easy to think of the implementation of strategy as a stage to worry about only once the strategy has been settled. This is not so, on several counts.

The nature of the strategy may be influenced by how easy it is to implement.

Example – implementation decides the strategy

When Jan Carlzon took over as head of SAS, the Scandinavian airline, in 1981, the centrepiece of his strategy was that SAS should become 'Europe's most punctual airline'. He chose something which could motivate every employee, since they could all contribute to its achievement. He didn't choose a strategy and then work out how to implement it – in large part what could be implemented decided his strategy.

In addition, as the last chapter discussed, the various stages of the strategy process may overlap. It may be possible to start trying out part of your strategy before the strategy as a whole is decided. This may provide lessons that improve the final strategy.

Unexpected factors may emerge while you are planning or implementing the strategy. You may find unexpected strategies emerging. All this may force you to go back to the strategy and revise it. Remember the example of Quicks on page 59, and how what appeared to be a recruitment problem turned into a problem of values.

Implementation is often thought of as a purely internal activity. In fact, implementation will be improved if users are involved. We go on to discuss this in more depth.

People

Many of the points in this section have already been made. They are repeated because implementation usually involves more people than were involved in creating the strategy. This section is divided into two. It begins with a discussion of the motivation that those involved in implementation need to have. It finishes with what top management needs to do in order to generate that motivation.

Leadership

Leadership is important throughout the process of developing strategy, but it is especially important at this stage. Having a strategy is not enough in itself to galvanise people into action. Implementation can feel like a hard grind after the excitement of making the strategy. Some strategies take a very long time to implement, and carrying out strategy often involves more people than were involved in making the strategy, so their commitment must be gained.

For all these reasons, the board of trustees and top management, especially the director, must lead. They must inspire, direct and do whatever it takes to communicate how important it is to carry out the strategy successfully. They must sustain this leadership throughout the implementation period. It must be clear each day that trustees and top management as a whole are determined that the strategy will happen, and that obstacles will be overcome.

At the beginning of implementation, the pace and extent of change are often unclear. For this reason, trustees and top management are often tempted to delay communicating the strategy. This rarely works, because it leaves room for rumour to generate fears greater than anything the truth can provide. News often leaks out in any case.

Trustees and top management should therefore convey the strategy to the rest of the organisation as soon as possible. Raise expectations, so that people are ready for change. However, do not raise them too high, in case disappointment leads to disillusion. Remember that those not already involved will be some way behind those who are, and will need to be brought up to date. Try to give everyone the 'big picture', so that they can relate it to changes in their own circumstances. Encourage people to think through what those changes will be, so that difficulties emerge as early as possible. Be prepared for an initial fall in morale, as people mourn the loss of old roles and see the disadvantages, before any of the benefits have been seen in practice. Be aware that people who are feeling disgruntled will look for ways to make their feelings known to trustees, top management and important stakeholders. Provide channels for people to express their feelings. Make sure that those who may be on the receiving end of this disgruntlement are not taken by surprise.

The people, political and project management skills needed to drive implementation through are different from those needed to make strategy. So larger organisations especially will need to decide whether the planner is the right person to be responsible for implementation. If they choose someone else, they must ensure that the planner is not seen either as having failed, or as having lost interest in the process.

Commitment

There are two forms of commitment that will influence the success of implementation. Commitment to the organisation was examined in the last chapter. This chapter looks at commitment to the strategy. This is different. If people's view of their organisation is threatened by a new strategy, they will have the first form of commitment, but not the second.

The main factors that cause people to be committed to a strategy are:

- understanding the strategy;
- feeling that it will enhance the organisation;
- a sense of excitement;
- 'owning' the strategy;
- feeling that their contribution will affect the success of implementation.

The first three factors depend primarily on how well the leadership and the planning group have communicated the strategy. Owning the strategy depends partly on communication, on whether the strategy has been put to people in terms of their language and concepts, but it depends mainly on their involvement in planning for implementation, as does the last factor.

The main factors that cause people *not* to be committed to a strategy are:

- vested interests are threatened;
- strategies take time that people think that they do not have;
- strategies take resources – meeting room space, photocopying, committee members', time, etc – for which there is always competition;
- strategies cost money to develop that many managers would prefer to spend on other things;
- strategies can run counter to the culture of the organisation;
- there can be a general lack of trust.

Do not be surprised if opposition emerges now that has not surfaced before. The demands on time, for instance, may during the making of strategy have seemed too far away to be a threat.

The nature and source of lack of commitment may not be what they first appear. Those with vested interests, for example, may shelter behind those with more respectable causes for concern.

Exercise 41 Force field analysis

This exercise will help you to understand the forces inhibiting and supporting change.

1 For your particular strategy, carry out a basic force field analysis, as described and illustrated in Appendix 1.

2 You can extend the analysis by taking the people involved (not all the forces will be people) and listing all the issues related to the change, eg change of job description. You can then note on a matrix of people and issues how each person is affected by each issue. This will guide you in deciding on which issues and which people to concentrate.

3 Page 123 of Chapter 6 discussed how to handle strategic alliances between stakeholders. It may be worth examining the alliances between the people involved in a change. Enter their names on both axes of a matrix and then fill in the matrix with the relationships between the people concerned. An example of this kind of relationship matrix is given below.

	Alice	Bill	Cheryl
Alice	–	mother/son	manager/team member
Bill	son/mother	–	friend
Cheryl	team member/ manager	friend	–

Once you have identified those who are uncommitted or opposed, it may help to work out how much power they have to stop or delay implementation. Here are some questions which will help you to examine the extent of this power. They apply both to an individual and to a group:

- How much status do they have in the organisation?
- To how much of the organisation's resources can they lay claim?
- Are they in key positions, eg on the most important committees?
- What are the symbols of power – what are the equivalents in your organisation to the key to the executive washroom?

How are you going to cope with the lack of commitment, on the basis of the information gathered so far? The use of that information is vital. A common failure is that managers always use the same approach, instead of suiting their approach to the problem. Avoiding the issue and hoping it will go away does not count, so there are six approaches:

- *Participation.* In addition to the advantages explained above, participation is especially valuable for those worried about loss of control or loss of face.
- *Acknowledgement.* Acknowledging people's concerns is an essential first step to reassure them that their voices will be heard, and that their problems will not be swept under a carpet of false consensus.
- *Support.* Support in the form of counselling or retraining is the best approach when people are anxious about their ability to change.
- *Negotiation.* Negotiation is often the way to tackle common threats felt by a group, if they cannot be dealt with by the other methods listed here.
- *Manipulation.* If the first four methods fail, the alternative to outright coercion is to use influence behind the scenes to undermine opposition.
- *Coercion.* Coercion should only be used, if at all, where speed is vital and no method of winning support for a change is likely to succeed.

The feeling of threat and the appropriate method of dealing with it will be influenced by the culture of the organisation. Think back to the classification of cultures on pages 39 to 41. A member of a task culture will expect more change and be less threatened by it than a member of a role culture. Coercion is more acceptable in a power culture than in a person culture, which expects one of the first four approaches above.

Accountability

People do not need only to be committed to the strategy. They need also to commit themselves to playing their part in its implementation. This means being held to account for how well they do. Leaders need either to state that they will hold people to account or, preferably, persuade people to hold themselves to account. Without a detailed plan, people may not be able to tell what it is they are supposed to be doing. Reward systems, discussed below, should reinforce accountability.

Accountability too often consists of criticism or punishment for anything short of success. Such sanctions encourage people to conceal mistakes and discourage risk taking. This reduces the commitment on which success depends. So remember that accountability need not involve sanctions at all. It may require no more than asking people to explain their results to an implementation review meeting.

The action plan

Once the strategy is decided, there is a strong temptation to proceed with it immediately. However, the longer the time spent in planning the implementation, the shorter the time that implementation will take. This section is an extended exercise devoted to preparing an action plan.

A detailed action plan is essential. In one survey of public and private sector organisations, half of the ten main difficulties with implementation were due to lack of planning. These were:

- implementation took longer than expected
- unexpected problems arose
- co-ordination of activities was ineffective
- training was inadequate
- key tasks were not defined in sufficient detail

The issue to resolve is the speed of implementation. A dress rehearsal, as suggested on page 135, may help to resolve this. Below are some additional factors to consider:

- What are the risks if the entire strategy is tried at once, and fails?
- If phasing in the strategy seems worthwhile, should the first phase be part of the strategy in the whole organisation, or the whole strategy in part of the organisation?
- If change depends on people outside the organisation, you may have to proceed stage by stage. One psychological experiment found that people were much more likely to accept a large billboard on their lawn if they had first been persuaded to take a much smaller board. Similarly, the police have persuaded local authorities to install surveillance cameras in town centres by installing their own cameras first.
- Changes in culture take a long time. The National Association of Development Education Centres (NADEC), for example, has been transformed into the Development Education Association to co-ordinate all development education. It brings together two groups with very different cultures. The development education centres are small, often 3–4 part-timers; opportunistic, accustomed to seeing a funding opportunity and going for it; and non-hierarchical. The second group is the aid agencies, much larger, more structured, with a mix of role and task cultures. The transformation needs to be step by step, so that the two groups get to know each other. Rather than go straight to the final structure, for example, an interim council was set up, with representatives of both parties.
- Organisations are inevitably turbulent during periods of great

change. But turbulence cannot be permanent – people need some stability in their lives, so ensure that there are periods of relative stability. If you have set yourself too much strategic change to achieve, you may have to delay implementing part of it until the initial changes have been digested.

- You cannot expect people to take on work over and above their normal duties for very long. You may have to choose between a swift and intensive effort, or a longer implementation period where the extra burden is spread to make it tolerable.

The first requirement of the action plan is to provide enough resources. This means: money, people, time, and technical expertise. It must also describe who is doing what, and by when.

Here is a procedure for developing an action plan:

- Assemble a working group for each major strategy. This spreads the workload. (Small voluntary organisations may need only one group.) Each group should involve those with most knowledge of the relevant area of work. You may want to include a few people from outside that area of work, who may be more objective and better able to raise difficult issues.

- Identify the strategies, objectives, critical success factors etc that apply to each working group. In a large organisation, where there are several working groups, it may help for the planning team to develop an objective tree. This involves taking each main objective and working out the secondary objectives which contribute to it. Then take each secondary objective and work out which objectives contribute to those. The result will be a hierarchy. Carry on until you have objectives relevant to the unit you are concerned with, such as the working group.

- Each group specifies:
  - The individual tasks needed to achieve the strategy. The more complex the strategy, the greater the need to break it down into small steps. The description of each task should start with an action verb (eg 'We will review the salary structure').

- The time each task should take.
- The people and other resources that each task should involve. The ways that people may be involved should be specified. They may be responsible either for making things happen or for support; or have the right either to approve change or to be kept informed.
- The implications for other strategies/working groups.

- Each group presents its work to the planning group for comment.

- Someone goes through the plans to identify tasks in strategy A that depend on tasks in strategy B having been achieved – in other words, draws up the critical path for the process.

- Combine the individual plans into an overall plan. This in particular shows all the tasks, month by month. Do not be put off by the fact that some strategies, such as changing the culture, will require several years to implement.

- The planning group then has a vital role in reviewing the plan to ensure co-ordination. The issues include:
  - Is the plan complete?
  - Are the key objectives/critical success factors likely to be achieved?
  - Are the timings realistic? Can the implementation period be shortened?
  - Is the critical path clear? This is the sequence of tasks that allows each task to be tackled after the other tasks that are pre-requisites for it have been accomplished. You cannot, for example, have the finance working group relying on a new recruit in six months' time if the personnel group has not planned to recruit anyone for a year.
  - Is it clear who is accountable for each task?
  - Are there some 'quick wins' (early results) for the sake of good morale and to keep expectation high?

Activities

The plan will cover two types of action. The first is using existing activities in different ways. The activity of fundraising, for instance, may be directed at different targets. The second action, however, is redesigning the activity itself. This means looking at how things are done just as much as at what is done. One American company looked at exactly how an invoice was produced and reduced the time it took from over $3^1/_2$ days to 30 minutes. Figure 7 shows the stages of the process. The diagrams represent the sequence of actions involved in producing an invoice. 'Hands on' means that work is going on, 'queue' that paper is waiting to be processed. The redesign involved reducing the actual work and eliminating the queueing.

Here are two ground rules for redesigning activities:

- Activities need people who are responsible for them. In all but the smallest voluntary organisations, people's responsibilities are within sections or departments. To manage activities you need people whose responsibility reaches through the walls between sections or departments.
- Be prepared to challenge long-held traditions and beliefs.

Examples – reducing work

Unnecessary work

The invoice processing above was one example. Another is from a company called Oryx. When it looked at work that didn't need to be done, it eradicated 25 per cent of all internal reports, reduced from 20 to 4 the number of signatures needed on requests to spend capital, and reduced from seven months to six weeks the time it took to produce the annual budget.

Work whose original purpose has disappeared

Segas (South Eastern Gas) had a policy of moving meters from inside houses to outside. This made it easier to read them and to

Figure 7 Flow charts of invoice production before and after redesign

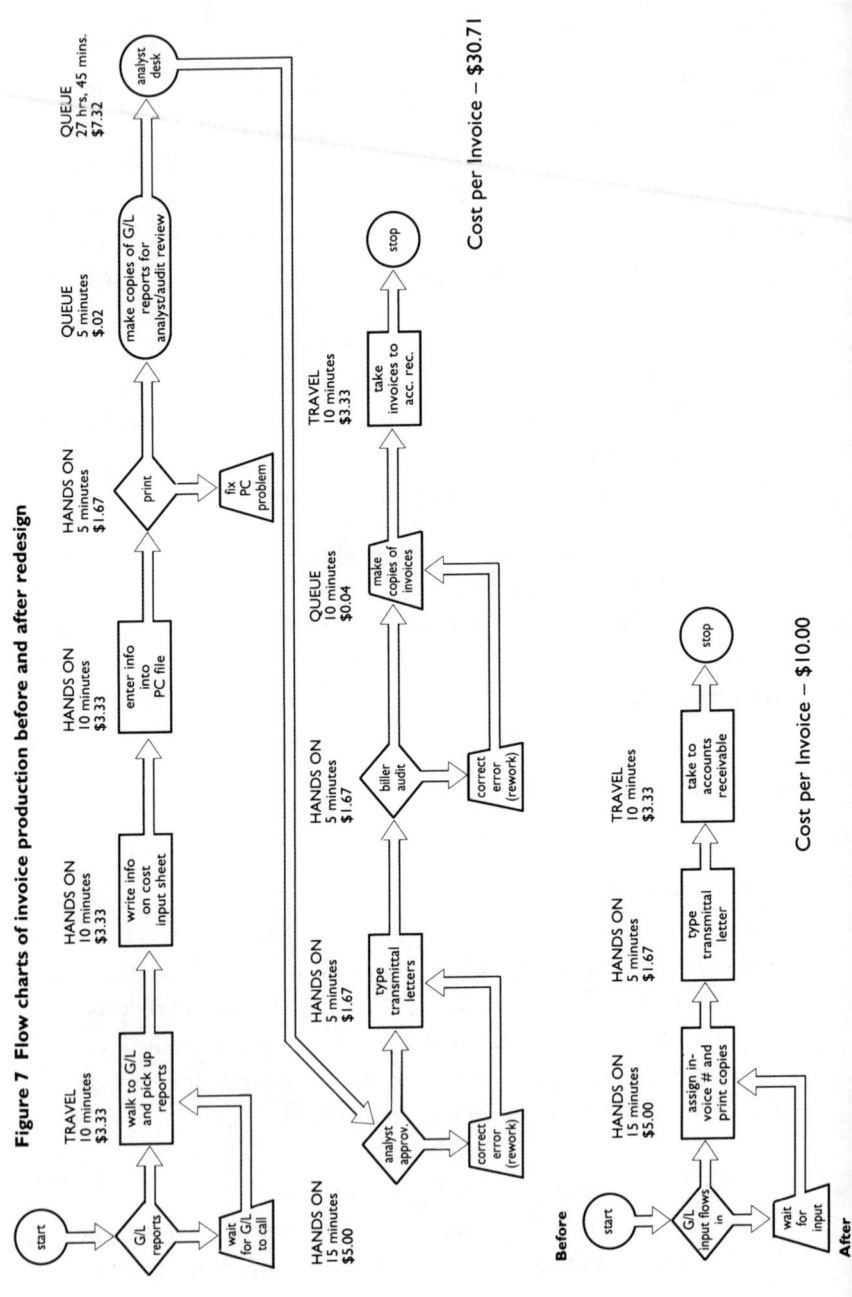

Cost per Invoice – $30.71

Cost per Invoice – $10.00

148

cut off supplies in an emergency. However, it had switched to reading meters less often and had found another way of cutting off supplies. When it realised this, the company stopped moving meters and saved itself a million pounds a year.

Duplication between departments
One company found that computer systems were being developed not only in the computer department, but also in the parts, service and engineering departments.

Measures and indicators

Why should you measure performance? All organisations need to check whether they are achieving their strategy, and hence achieving their purpose. Voluntary organisations need to do this even more than for-profit organisations, which can tell whether they are making a profit from their accounts.

Demonstrating achievement in this way is powerful motivation. This is true for all stakeholders, but especially for staff. Buried in daily routine, they can easily miss the fact that many small improvements add up to significant gains.

Measurement may also be essential to be able to demonstrate achievement regularly to funders.

You cannot find measures if you do not know what you are trying to measure, so clear objectives are essential. The case study on Lewisham Theatre at the end of this section illustrates this point well.

Two terms are used in this chapter to signify what is measured: measures and indicators. Indicators are a particular type of measure: they are measures that can be precisely quantified. It follows that measures may be quantitative or qualitative.

One of the very hardest decisions to make in strategic planning is what to measure. This section explains what the options are, looks at the questions that will enable you to select between options, and shows you where to find measures for that option.

There are three main options. You can measure one or more of:

- *inputs* – the resources committed to an activity;
- *outputs* – the immediate results of the activity;
- *outcomes* – the impacts of the activity on the organisation's goals or objectives.

The example of a training course can be used to illustrate the difference between the options. The inputs, the resources, are the time and money spent. One output is the course itself. The course has an impact on skills, attitudes and behaviour, which in turn have an impact on the performance of the organisation. The impact on performance is an outcome.

This example also shows how measurement becomes harder as inputs turn into outcomes. The inputs of a course are straightforward to measure. So is the output in terms of the course being run. The output in terms of enhanced skills is harder. The outcome, the impact on performance, is harder again. Performance is often affected by changes in the outside world – in government regulations for example. Even if the effect of these can be isolated, improvements in performance within the organisation are often team efforts. Even if the contribution of individuals can be identified, the contribution of a course that may have taken place six months ago is hard to estimate.

Policing also illustrates the variation in ease of measurement. A force may increase its inputs, the number of police on the beat, for example. Outputs may be measurable, for example the number of arrests. But the outcome is much more difficult, with the difficulty depending on how general the goals are. If the goal is to reduce crime, it may be possible to tell how effective extra patrols have been. If the goal is to reduce the fear of crime, only a fairly elaborate survey by questionnaire could establish whether the goal had been met.

The differences between inputs, outputs and outcomes can be shown as a spectrum (Figure 8). Moving along the spectrum from left to right, from inputs towards outputs, the characteristics on the left reduce and those on the right grow.

Figure 8 The Measurement Spectrum

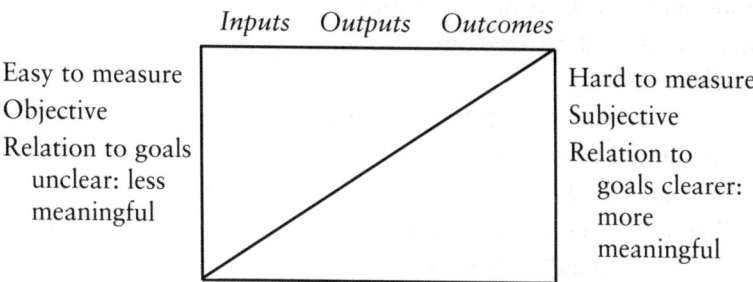

Inputs   Outputs   Outcomes

Easy to measure
Objective
Relation to goals
    unclear: less
    meaningful

Hard to measure
Subjective
Relation to
    goals clearer:
    more
    meaningful

Twenty years ago, the starting point for an issue such as evaluating a course would have been inputs, such as the number of places, on the grounds that anything else was too difficult. The starting point in this book is outcomes, because what counts is whether the organisation meets its goals.

Below is a series of questions, in three categories, to help you to choose which options to measure. You can ask the questions either in relation to your overall strategy or in relation to individual strategies. Each question is discussed in turn. When you have read the discussion, tick against each question in Table 4 whether in your case it suggests that you should measure inputs (I), outputs (OT), or outcomes (OE).

Table 4 Choosing Measurement Options

Question	I	OT	OE
Category A: the outcome			
1 Can you define the outcome?			
2 Can you control whether the outcome is being achieved?			
3 Can you ask the beneficiaries whether the outcome is being achieved?			
4 Is achieving the outcome what really matters, irrespective of the contribution made by your organisation?			

| Question | I | OT | OE |

Category B: the links between inputs and outputs and between outputs and outcomes

5 Are the relationships between input and output and between output and outcome clear?

6 How long does it take to turn inputs into outputs and outputs into outcomes?

Category C: indicators

7 Can measures and indicators be found?

8 Are indicators likely to be misused?

Category A: the outcome

The more 'yes' answers there are to questions in this category, the easier it is to measure outcomes.

1 *Can the outcome be defined?*

Voluntary organisations often feel that their goals are intrinsically unclear. The Civic Trust, for example, has launched a campaign on the quality of life in urban areas. It feels that the influences on quality of life are so many and varied that it cannot set specific goals for the campaign. This view should however be put to the test. For instance, US hospitals, according to management guru Peter Drucker, usually say, 'Our mission is health care'. He disagrees: 'The hospital does not take care of health; the hospital takes care of illness.' He helped a hospital to think through the mission of its emergency room. The result was: 'To give assurance to the afflicted'. Drucker comments, 'It turned out that in a good emergency room, the function is to tell eight out of ten people that there is nothing wrong that a good night's sleep won't take care of.'

Some missions do make a successful outcome very hard to define. This is especially true if they are built around abstract principles like liberty and equality. The mission of the New Economics Foundation is 'to develop and promote new economic approaches which can help build an economy that is sustainable, socially just, and able to deliver a high quality of life for all.' Except in the most general sense, what a sustainable and socially just economy would look like is unclear.

2 *Can you control whether the outcome is being achieved?*
Even if you can define the outcome, you may not be able to control whether it is achieved. A farmer can define what a successful harvest is, but cannot control the weather and so cannot control success.

When the Valleys Programme was launched in Wales in 1988, its key economic objective was to reduce unemployment by 25–30,000. The recession soon made this hopelessly unrealistic. Instead of monitoring the outcome it might have been better to monitor the output, the number of the jobs that the programme itself was to create.

3 *Can you ask the beneficiaries whether the outcome is being achieved?*
It is sometimes impossible to ask those for whom the strategy is designed what their views are. The RSPCA cannot poll animals (animals are beneficiaries rather than users, hence the term). The Society for the Preservation of the Unborn Child cannot question foetuses. Often, however, it is possible. How to consult beneficiaries and other stakeholders is explained below.

4 *Is achieving the outcome what really matters irrespective of the contribution made by your organisation?*
If so, this is what you will focus on. If, however, you need to justify your existence, you will want to be able to demonstrate your contribution, by measuring inputs and outputs and showing their link to outcomes.

Category B: the links between inputs and outputs, and between outputs and outcomes

5 *Are the relationships between input and output and between output and outcome clear?*

The US hospital emergency room discussed above set a performance target, which is that everybody who comes in is seen by a qualified person in less than a minute. The target relates to inputs – to the resources used for the activity. This is partly because it is easier to measure than the outcome, which would be the degree of assurance felt by the afflicted person. But the main reason for relating the target to inputs is that there is a close relationship between inputs and outcomes. If someone who comes to the emergency room is looked after immediately by a qualified person, the chances are that she or he will feel reassured.

Whether the relationship is clear depends not only on whether it exists, but also on whether it is understood. The police, for example, have done a lot of work to understand the relationship between speed of response to emergency calls and public satisfaction with policing. They found that rapid response does not affect satisfaction, but that a slow response, eg over an hour, increases dissatisfaction.

So if there is a close and well understood relationship between inputs and outcome you can probably afford to measure inputs. This would imply a clear relationship both between inputs and outputs, and between outputs and outcomes. If only the second of these relationships was well defined, you would probably measure outputs.

For example, suppose that some of your staff were being sent on personal development courses in order to enhance their self-esteem and self-confidence. It might not be clear what the effect of any one course was, but very clear that increased self-confidence leads to improved performance. In that case, self-confidence, the output, is the option to measure, eg by questionnaire.

Exercise 42 Understanding the relationships between indicators

This exercise will help you to understand the relationships between input, output and outcome indicators.

One question that citizens are said to be interested in under the Citizens Charter is 'Are parks kept free of dog's mess?' One indicator suggested is the number of dog wardens. This of course is an input measure. What do you think is the relationship between inputs and outcomes in this case?

Possible answer: it obviously depends on how effective the wardens are. An output measure such as the number of hours spent in the park each week would be harder to calculate but would be a better guide to the outcome. It would probably only be practicable to measure the outcome itself if citizens reported dirty parks. This could probably be relied upon only if reporting was made very easy and if people believed that reporting would lead to swift action.

6 *How long does it take to turn inputs into outputs and outputs into outcomes?*

If it takes a long time for outputs to turn into outcomes, measure outputs. If it takes a long time to turn inputs into outputs, measure inputs as well. This is because remedial action may be too slow if you only look at outcomes.

Take fundraising as an example. If it takes a long time for charitable trusts to process your applications (your outputs), you need to monitor the number of applications so that you are not caught out by, say, failing to obtain a grant that you expected. If it also takes a long time to prepare an application, you need to measure the inputs, the resources that you are putting in to preparing applications.

Category C: indicators

7 Can measures and indicators be found?

Finding measures and indicators is usually harder for outcomes than for inputs and outputs. As stated before, however, what at first appears impossible may prove to be merely difficult. Here are two examples:

- The director of the Cleveland Museum uses 'repeat sales' as a measure. He means by this the number of people who come in out of the rain and are then inspired to come back as regular visitors.
- Alvin Toffler of *Future Shock* fame wrote an article called 'The Art of Measuring the Arts'. His criteria for cultural excellence included: technically outstanding; artists that include people of genius; and results that are consistently applauded abroad. He then suggested indicators for each one. Technical merit could be judged in the way that pianists are scored in competitions. Geniuses can be defined partly through consensus and partly through objective measures such as the number of citations by other artists and awards won.

You may think this is taking the concept too far, but the point is that indicators can almost always be found.

Here is a more down to earth example. How do you measure the helpfulness of library staff? One solution is to use a partial measure for which there is an indicator, such as the speed with which requests for new books are processed.

There are cases where inputs are hard to measure. The police, for example, claim to have allocated almost all their costs between their core functions, such as public safety and traffic management. A constable on the beat, however, has no idea which of these functions she or he will be called on to perform.

8 Are indicators likely to be misused?

When using indicators, precisely quantified measures, it is easy to assume that numbers and decimal points imply accuracy and precision. This may well not be the case. At a seminar on indicators at the Royal Society of Arts, a member of the audience quoted the saying most often used to justify indicators: 'What gets measured gets done'. 'Oh no,' another member of the audience retorted, 'What gets measured gets fiddled.'

When outcomes cannot be measured, the choice tends to fall on measures of outputs. This is because they can at least be measured and usually seem to have some relation to the final objective. These are particularly prone to abuse. This is because they replace larger goals and become the standard that motivates behaviour in the organisation.

Here are two examples of the dangers:

- One important measure in the National Health Service is throughput, the number of days it takes a patient to go through the system for a particular treatment. The danger is that too much attention is then paid to efficiency, and not enough to whether the patient benefited from the treatment.
- At the time of writing, the police are concerned that performance related pay will be introduced and that it will be related to, for instance, the number of arrests. As stated above, the link between arrests and the overall objectives of the police is unclear. Beyond this, however, such an approach could create a quota system that encouraged police officers to make their quota of arrests and then slacken off, and discouraged officers who were good at crime prevention and so needed to make fewer arrests.

Choosing measures

From working through the previous section, you should have been able to decide which of the options you wanted to measure. The purpose of this section is to help you to choose appropriate measures.

There are several criteria for what makes a good measure. There may be trade-offs between them. The criteria are:

- The information should be timely, relevant, easy and above all cheap to collect and produce.
- The measure should be easy to understand.
- Sometimes it helps to find indicators that can be compared across a range of departments or organisations. This means ensuring a common definition – eg not all police forces include arrests for drunkenness in their arrest figures.
- Will the measure change frequently?
- Will the measure lead to action?
- What do users think is a good measure? (This is often ignored.)
- Is the measure acceptable to stakeholders? There may be conflicting interests between stakeholders, in which case you may need to use the methods of conflict resolution described in Chapter 6.
- Can the data be easily entered into a computer and manipulated?

If there are a large number of measures, there are two other requirements. It should be clear what the key measures are. You cannot expect your trustee board to monitor 35 measures; you should recommend the few key measures. The YHA, for example, has three critical measures: overnight stays, membership numbers, and meal sales. The measures should if possible be arranged in a hierarchy. This makes it clear which the key ones are and makes it much easier to absorb and use the others, because their inter-relationship is clear. A housing association, for example, might look at the proportion of repairs carried out within a specified period of time. It might then break those repairs down into those posing a health or safety risk; those disrupting residents' comfort; and non-urgent repairs.

Examples – inappropriate indicators

London Underground
In 1990, London Underground's monthly figures were showing most lines operating at nearly 100 per cent of scheduled mileage, at a time when rush-hour performance was not very good. This stemmed from the way the indicator was calculated.

Some trains were so delayed that they ran in off-peak periods. Off-peak scheduled mileage was then over 100 per cent, balancing out the below 100 per cent performance in the rush-hour, when performance mattered.

Royal Mail

In 1988 the Royal Mail had a dispute with its Users Association. The Users Association claimed that only 70 per cent of first-class mail arrived the day after posting. The Royal Mail claimed a far higher figure, but it turned out that its measure was from the point the letter was date stamped to the point that it was ready for delivery. The time before date stamping and before completing delivery was excluded. It then took the Mail 15 months to acquire true data, which showed that the users had been right. The Mail had measured what was easy to measure, at the price of relevance.

Federal Aviation Administration

The US Federal Aviation Administration gives an airline credit for being on time based on when it touches down. So if the airline then leaves its passengers sitting in the plane on the tarmac for three hours, its record does not suffer.

Delivery to customer requirements

One company always delivered on the due date, but was losing customers. The reason was that customers wanted the product even sooner. The company should have been monitoring not 'delivered as promised' but 'delivered to customer requirements'.

Monitoring stock levels

A pharmaceutical company had as its measure of whether it was satisfying its customers 'delivery within 24 hours'. This reduced sales. Wholesalers did not bother to re-order until they ran out because they could get new supplies so quickly. While they were temporarily out of stock chemists bought rival products. The measure should have been to keep wholesalers always in stock.

Measures can worsen the tendency to see an organisation as a series of separate compartments. One way round this is to define indicators which are ratios of two other indicators, each from different 'compartments'. The role of such ratios is to stimulate thought rather than to guide policy, since the relationship between the two component indicators is unlikely to be clear. The Sustainable Seattle Indicators Project, for example, includes a series of 'provocative indicators'. One is the ratio of McDonald's restaurants to vegetarian restaurants.

Standards

Standards define the level of performance that represents success or failure. Their value is in making it easier to interpret the measure. An example is Rank Xerox's target to reduce customer dissatisfaction to zero from 7 per cent within two years.

The simplest and safest way of setting a standard is to compare your present performance with your own past performance and establish a target for improvement. Less safe is comparing your present performance with another organisation's present performance. For instance, one analysis of housing associations' accounts showed that net rent arrears varied from 30 days' rent due to 1 day's. The trouble is that this does not just measure the effectiveness of the housing association. High arrears may be at least partly due to delays in the direct payment of housing benefit by local authorities.

Standards can be very difficult to define. One indicator for education under the Citizen's Charter is how full schools are. This indicator, however, serves two objectives that pull in opposite directions. To be efficient, schools should be as full as possible. To provide parental choice, there must be spare places. So a single standard indicating how full a school ought to be is impossible to define.

Some standards are imposed on an organisation from outside. In such cases, the organisation should also develop its own standards, so that it can gauge whether it is being successful in its own terms as well as in someone else's.

A further difficulty is that in order to set a standard for an indicator of the success of a strategy, it helps to know what would have happened if the policy had not been applied. Suppose, for instance, that burglaries have fallen by 5 per cent in an area where the police have carried out a special exercise, known as Operation Bumblebee. The degree of success this represents depends on whether burglaries would otherwise have risen by 20 per cent or fallen by 10 per cent. You will need to judge whether previous years or other areas provide a good guide to this.

Benchmarking

One of the criteria of a good indicator above was that it would enable comparison between organisations. A technique that has become popular in the business world in recent years is benchmarking. This means comparing your performance with that of other organisations which have the reputation of being the best in the field. Any comparison with a similar organisation would be valuable.

Examples – benchmarking

DEA

The newly formed Development Education Association compares itself with the Council for Environmental Education (CEE), a similar organisation but in a field different enough to avoid competition. Each has observer status with the other. From the CEE the DEA has learnt a great deal about the nature of the service that its members would want and about constructive lobbying of government.

Glasgow

In 1990 Glasgow City Council devised indices to measure the prosperity of European cities. They ranked 30 European cities of similar size in four divisions. Glasgow came out bottom of division three. They used the ranking to set themselves the target of reaching the top of the second division by the end of the century.

Ford
Ford Motor Company was very proud of having reduced the number of people in its purchase ledger department to 500. It compared itself with a similar sized Japanese firm and found that the latter had 50 people in the same department.

Choosing measures of stakeholder satisfaction

As discussed earlier, organisations need to measure how well they are doing in satisfying their stakeholders. In the case of conventional businesses, the task is simplified because customers are seen as the major, although not the only, stakeholder. Customer satisfaction surveys are well established.

Example – customer satisfaction survey

Rank Xerox has been doing regular customer satisfaction surveys since 1985. By 1991 the company estimated that 7 per cent of its customer base was dissatisfied. Its target was to reduce this to zero by 1993. A percentage of the pay of all of Rank Xerox's 4,000 UK employees is tied to the achievement of customer satisfaction targets. The more senior the employee is, the bigger the percentage.

The case study on Lewisham Theatre below discusses customer surveys for a non-profit-making organisation.

For voluntary organisations the position is more complex, because there are several important stakeholders. But again, this makes the task difficult, not impossible. Here is the example of Traidcraft, which, although a business, is not conventional.

Example – measuring stakeholder satisfaction

Traidcraft's mission is 'to establish a just trading system which expresses the principles of love and justice fundamental to the Christian faith.' When trying to measure how far it had succeeded, the organisation started with its four stakeholders: producer partners in the third world; consumers and the wider public; Traidcraft staff and volunteers; and shareholders. The choice of indicators took into account the views of stakeholders. In the case of producer partners the indicators covered three areas:

- Producer remuneration – eg how much of Traidcraft's income was paid to primary producers.
- Community effects – eg workers' status in the community.
- Quality of partnership relations – eg how far Traidcraft had learnt and institutionalised lessons about the situation of producer partners.

All these methods have to be used with great care. Surveys of the fear of crime, for instance, show much higher levels of fear if a particularly brutal crime has recently been reported. Complaints are an increasingly popular measure of the views of users, but should also be treated with caution. The media view the increasing number of complaints to British Rail as a sign of a deteriorating rail network. It is just as likely to mean the opposite. More people may be complaining because BR publicises the opportunity to do so more than it previously did, and also because customers now feel they are more likely to receive a response and perhaps compensation. Both factors could be a sign of improvement.

Example – performance indicators for Lewisham Theatre

Lewisham Theatre is in a mixed area of inner suburbia in south-east London. Lewisham Council featured in the 1992 BBC2 series *Town Hall,* in which the theatre was shown hosting a show for pensioners.

The theatre was opened by the Council in 1932 as a *palais de danse*. More recent bookings include comedians Freddie Starr and Hale and Pace. In common with many other local entertainment venues, the theatre may become a charitable trust over the next few years.

Council members and officers are the theatre's most important group of stakeholders, since the Council provides a significant subsidy. Councillors' main interests tend to be in economy and efficiency rather than effectiveness in achieving objectives. Other major external stakeholders include the paying customers, the artists, and the people who hire the theatre for their own events. There is a hirers' forum for the 30 hirers who normally book the theatre at least once a year.

When the theatre's strategy was reviewed in 1991 there was no written artistic policy. Staff therefore had no framework within which to develop performance indicators. Those which were chosen were *ad hoc* and variable.

In 1992 the Council's director of leisure services laid down the following seven main indicators for the theatre.

1 Net subsidy per attendance
2 Net subsidy per head of population
3 Number of public performances
4 Tickets sold as percentage of capacity
5 Concessionary users as percentage of usage
6 Usage in relation to Council's target groups; these covered women, children and black audiences
7 Complaints/compliments per 1,000 users

Exercise 43 Evaluating performance indicators

Consider the performance indicators for Lewisham Theatre listed above.

1 What is your view of these indicators?

2 Can you think of any others which could be used instead or in addition?

Possible answers:

- Having a few key indicators means that they are easy to grasp.
- The indicators are heavily financial, reflecting the priorities of the stakeholder who imposed them. The fact that they were imposed reduces ownership in the organisation and makes it more likely that the results will be 'fiddled'.
- Other indicators should cover the artistic objectives.

Exercise 44 Relating indicators to objectives

Consider the following statement of artistic objectives for Lewisham Theatre, a shortened version of those in the 1991 business plan.

- Enriching the lives of the people of Lewisham as the principal entertainments venue for Lewisham and the surrounding region.
- Providing quality product and quality service.
- Access – extending the range of those benefiting from the arts and entertainments.
- Cultural diversity.

Answer the following questions:

1 Can these objectives be measured?

2 Which indicators would you use for each objective? Are the seven indicators given in the example sufficient?

Possible answers:

- The first question is whether 'enrichment' is a valid objective. Anecdotal evidence suggests that it does represent the feeling of the people of Lewisham about the theatre. It would be possible to survey different categories of user. They could, for example, be asked which council services most enrich their lives.
- Measurement is easier, however, if 'enrichment' is broken down into its component parts, which is in effect what the other three objectives do.
- Regarding the second objective, only the indicator of complaints/compliments is directly related to quality. Other possible indicators are:

  - reviews in the local press
  - new work as a percentage of the total
  - satisfaction levels of hirers
  - the existence of public forums, eg a friends organisation
  - qualitative assessment by theatre management

- For access, possible indicators are:

  - percentage of work directed at attracting new audiences
  - range of different arts represented
  - total number of people through the building
  - public awareness

  However, none of these is entirely satisfactory. Measuring access really requires a user survey to measure how many patrons were new to the theatre and whether they would return.

- The issue of cultural diversity is well covered by the indicator of usage in relation to target groups.

The example and exercises above will have helped you to understand how to set objectives so that effective indicators can be found.

Further points to note are:

- Indicators will be meaningless unless the objectives – what is to be measured – are clear.
- Many of the best measures in this example involve asking users of the theatre for their views. The theatre has at present no market research budget with which to do this. The question is whether it can beg or borrow resources; using a college student to do a survey is one possibility.

Systems

This section briefly covers systems for management information and for performance appraisal. Only those aspects that support implementation are covered. It also gives some guidance on financial systems, since strategy cannot be considered in isolation from resources.

Management information

Management information systems (MIS) are often assumed to require a computer and expensive software; this is not necessarily the case. The suggested approach is to work out what information you need, and then how to provide it.

The sections above on measures and planning should have made you aware of what information you require. List this, and also list against it the information already available. This specification tells you what information you still need to acquire. Take care that information on your environment is covered. This is easily forgotten, since it is not automatically generated by the activities of the organisation. Monitoring implementation is covered in the next chapter; that will tell you when the information is required. The criteria for information are the same as those above for measures: it should be timely, accurate, and so on.

There are two particular requirements for an MIS. First, if there is a lot of data, it should be capable of summarising it. The average adult can handle seven pieces of information at one time. Management reports too often contain so much information that it is impossible to pick out the important from the trivial. We have already pointed out that the ease of implementation is related to the quality of strategy. Likewise, the more that indicators have been arranged into a hierarchy, the easier it is to construct a manageable report. Remember the value of diagrams and graphics in making information easier to absorb.

The second requirement is flexibility. There is a story of a US component manufacturer that set up an elaborate database of machinists living up to half an hour away from its factory in New Jersey. Its cost structure changed so that in order to stay competitive it needed to move to somewhere like Taiwan. In such circumstances there is a danger that the information system drives the strategy, not the other way around. The information system itself needs regular review to check that what it contains is still relevant.

Performance appraisal

Earlier parts of this chapter have discussed accountability and the need for individual actions to have individual people responsible for them. These people should be appraised on how successfully they have carried out these actions.

The question arises of how success should be acknowledged. Business books discussing this topic usually talk in terms of payment for results. That may well be inappropriate for some voluntary organisations. They may lack the resources, or payment by results may be against their ethos.

You need to understand the relative importance that staff give to rewards and recognition. One example of recognition might be public thanks by the committee or by the trustees. Another example might be to give people work that is particularly dear to their heart. This is all part of building a culture that values the successful completion of tasks.

Financing your future

Whenever Napoleon's marshals came out with great plans for moving against Prussia or Spain or elsewhere, Napoleon would listen silently and then ask, 'How many horses does it require?'

Strategy today cannot be considered in isolation from resources. At the same time, you do not have to be a financial wizard to plan. This is not a book about financial or business planning. We would recommend that the reader seeking information on making financial projections and other issues refers to Martin and Smith's book on business planning in this NCVO series. At the same time, no book on strategy can ignore the financial issues which are so vital for voluntary organisations.

Below we identify key financial issues that bear on strategy. We suggest ways in which this book can be used to help you find solutions.

Assessing resources

The 1992 Charities Act has provided added impetus for tightening up financial management in voluntary organisations. A major benefit of improved financial systems and control for organisations contemplating strategic planning is that a much improved financial picture of the organisation's health can be obtained.

The income and expenditure account provides a picture of how the organisation has performed against original budget projections. The balance sheet offers one view of the assets and liabilities of the organisation. The funds flow statement can be important in showing sources of investment and loans. The accounting policies reveal how the organisation treated its financial data to arrive at the information contained in those accounts and statements.

All four can prove to be essential sources of information for strategic planning. They assist you in understanding where your organisation is for the exercises in Chapter 3. They provide information which you can use and update for devising strategic options as set out in Chapter 5. They may indicate policy or procedural barriers to change that need to be overcome or incorporated, as set out in Chapter 6. They will lay down measures and indicators of performance as explained in this chapter. Finance officers will tend to stress the importance of these sources of information. We would want to sound a note of caution, however. These documents provide a picture of what has happened in the past, not a guide to the future.

Obtaining resources

The issue of how to avoid dependence and yet survive is a critical one for all voluntary organisations. We know many managers and staff who are enormously adept at making applications and securing funds from diverse sources. The skills displayed are invaluable to the development of the voluntary sector, but they tend not to be strategic.

A significant danger this raises is that the organisation will hit an upper limit for its funding. The organisation's sources of funding will have been expanded to its limit and it will find itself short of money with no other sources of funding ready to yield funds for immediate needs. The organisation may survive the crisis that follows but its staffing levels, its activities and the users of its services will suffer.

The organisation's capacity to deliver its mission will be greatly impeded if it has insufficient funds. Its will to deliver its mission will also be in question. Developing a funding and fundraising strategy as part of the overall strategic planning exercise is a necessity, not an add on. This requires the organisation to:

- Undertake an assessment of its internal capacities and will to deliver a fundraising strategy. Are the trustees and senior management committed? How do other staff and volunteers in the organisation see the process? What are the information resources of the organisation that can be mobilised? Chapters 3, 5 and 6 provide a number of tools and techniques to enable you to answer these questions.

- Develop a case for funds that is rooted in the mission, vision and values of the organisation. Special projects for which you are seeking funding need to show how they contribute to these ends and what value they add for the whole of the organisation. Chapters 4 and 5 can assist you in developing the core of the case, and in providing a basis for assessing the value of projects.
- Research and test the propositions of the case for funding. The assessment provided by external stakeholders is a major test for the organisation to see how fast it has learnt and can learn from a changing environment. The first part of Chapter 6 considers these issues in some depth.
- Pull together an implementation strategy that is realistic in the resources that will be committed to it and includes clear measures of performance. This chapter has given practical advice in this area.

Integrating financial planning with strategic planning

Whether it is recognised as such, your organisation will already have some financial planning processes. The most obvious example of this is the construction of the budget. As these processes deal with such critical issues, we would advise you to see that the financial planning process is integrated within the framework of strategic planning. It should become seen as the financial expression of how the strategic objectives of the organisation are going to be delivered.

A popular suggestion (rarely acted on) to integrate finances with strategy is a zero based budgeting exercise. The ability to assess performance more closely has encouraged interest in more radical approaches to financial analysis and budget construction. The significance of zero based budgeting is that it is a form of budgeting in which expenditure is estimated as if the organisation is being started from scratch. It involves a reassessment of the best way to allocate money in order to achieve objectives.

Estimate the resource implications of strategic change

Three factors require particular attention:

- overall resource requirements
- fit with existing resources
- fit with future resources and commitments

One way of assessing the implications would be to consider each of these factors against each element of your organisation's value chain. Set out and check the assumptions on which costing is based (eg price of service – on what basis are overheads calculated?). Look at the material on the chain in Chapter 5.

It is important in addition to consider the resource implications in the short, medium and long term. In each case, you need to check the basis of the assumptions that you are making about the cost of change. Do not be surprised if you change your assumptions in the process.

Action points

- If people feel threatened by the strategy, decide what approach you will take to deal with their fears.
- If implementation of part of the strategy is in doubt because of resistance, use the techniques recommended to work out who you need to involve or persuade.
- Look for ways of involving users.
- Develop an action plan.
- Review your activities, if this seems worthwhile.
- Develop measures and indicators to monitor performance.
- If appropriate, develop benchmark comparisons with other organisations.
- Align your management information, performance appraisal and financial systems with your strategy.

Chapter 8
Sustaining the Momentum

This chapter covers the final steps in the strategy process. It is about three ways of sustaining the momentum. First, it is about monitoring the process of implementation described in Chapter 7 to ensure that the strategy is carried out. Nothing is more demoralising than to feel that the result of so much hard work is gathering dust in a drawer.

Secondly, it is about how the act of monitoring implementation can be used to motivate people. This can in turn improve the quality of implementation – a virtuous circle.

Thirdly, we emphasise that strategic planning does not end when you have finished implementing your strategy. The earth keeps turning, and organisations need to keep up. You will simply have finished one cycle. The results should feed back into the next cycle. This is the iteration described in Chapter 1. The more often you repeat the process, the easier it should get.

The final section of the chapter is to encourage first-timers who have just finished reading the book and are suffering from a myriad of doubts.

Monitoring

Monitoring is essential to ensure that you stay on course. When the strategy is set and the action plan written it is tempting to breathe a sigh of relief and move on to other things. If you do this, however, you risk jeopardising all the hard work you have put in so far. Regular monitoring makes plans flexible. Small adjustments to the plan when things go wrong can keep the strategy valid. Without review, the strategy may become bogged down, or drift so far off course that there is nothing to do but start again. Monitoring also has the positive benefit of providing evidence of good results, which is good for morale and so helps produce further results.

A simple approach to monitoring is the four Rs: regularity, review, responsibility, and results.

Regularity

Regular review is the first essential to make sure that the strategy isn't quietly forgotten about or buried. This should not be less often than every six months – quarterly is preferable.

Continuous review is also possible. A list can be displayed of the steps towards implementation. It can be updated to show which actions have been completed and which are overdue.

Review

You may want to choose a focus for the review. You may want to concentrate on particular strategies. Other possibilities include:

- Are the objectives being met?
- How are stakeholders being affected by the strategy?
- Is the strategy fully understood, within the organisation and perhaps by stakeholders?

The commitment to regular review is indeed essential, but the quality of the review is also vital. This in turn requires two processes to be decided upon: the process of gathering the information and presenting it; and the process for the review meeting itself.

Gathering and presenting the information
- The ease with which the right information can be gathered and collected depends very much on the effort put into identifying goals and indicators, described in Chapter 7.

- Have goals and targets been met? If not, why? Would a gap analysis help to show what remains to be done? Don't forget to include by-products, things good or bad that you did not mean to achieve resulting from emergent strategies. Look especially for tasks or strategies that are complete.
- Summarise the tasks to be carried out between this review meeting and the next.
- The paperwork should be brief. If possible it should be no more than one side of A4. It should certainly be no more than two sides.
- Don't forget to include relevant information about what is happening outside the organisation.
- Pay attention to the language. What language will be easiest for the stakeholders represented at the meeting to understand?

The review meeting
- Pick a different focus for each meeting.
- If the review is part of a wider management or board of trustees meeting, try to see that the review is taken early in the meeting, when people are still fresh; but not first, when they may not have 'warmed up'.
- Brief the chair.
- Prepare a clear set of questions to which you need answers.
- Make any presentations short, preferably no more than ten minutes.
- Where decisions are needed, suggest options.
- Make sure that there is clarity on the decisions the meeting has reached, especially on the next steps.

Example – a review meeting agenda

The Women's Environmental Network has a six-monthly review meeting called a 'weather report', open to all staff. (The executive director thinks the attendance would halve if she called it a strategy review.) The agenda is:

- Meditation
- What's the weather? People describe how they feel in terms of the weather – sunny, calm etc
- Appreciations – people provide feedback to each other, without interruption
- New information
- Criticisms – but only if you can provide a constructive alternative
- Puzzles, notes and queries
- Wishes, hopes and dreams, for individuals and the organisation
- Planning to achieve these wishes, hopes and dreams

Responsibility

Somebody, or more than one person, needs to take responsibility for carrying out the steps in the section above. Who is involved, and what they are to do, should be clearly agreed.

Like the commitment to review, this is necessary but not sufficient. The responsibility is unlikely to be properly discharged if it has been allocated, or even accepted, by someone who already has more than enough to occupy them for all their time. The organisation must acknowledge that if they take on something else, part of their existing work will have to be cancelled, switched or deferred.

Results

The results of the review need to be communicated to the organisation at large. It may be simplest to use your normal methods of communication, but a special 'strategy bulletin' may have more impact.

The importance of communicating was stressed in Chapter 7. So was the need for 'quick wins' – early results. If those quick wins can be followed by others at regular intervals, so much the better. Nothing motivates like success.

Successes will stay in people's minds and motivate them for longer if they are celebrated. Celebration may not come naturally to those who are task oriented. Those to whom it will occur, probably the more people oriented, should be encouraged.

What do you do if things are not on course? First, be honest: don't ignore the difficulty. Resist the temptation to blame the outside world. Contingencies in the plan should take care of most unexpected changes. Secondly, stop and think. There is a tendency to say 'strategy A has failed, so let's try strategy B'. Unless you understand why the first strategy failed, the new strategy is also likely to fail. Look for the cause, first of all within the organisation.

There are two possibilities. The strategy may be all right, but the process of implementation has gone wrong. Check this first. Some likely causes are listed in Chapter 7 on page 144. Others may be a failure of leadership or communication; less ability within the organisation to cope with change than was expected; stakeholders being less supportive than expected. Look out especially for vicious circles. Suppose, for example, that the initial drop in morale and performance was greater than expected. Managers might then push harder for results, leading to a further drop in morale.

The second possibility is that the strategy is truly off course. Review each element of the strategy. It should be possible to identify at which level the difficulty has arisen.

Examples – failed strategies

NEF

In 1992 the New Economics Foundation noticed that it was falling behind its target for supporter recruitment. This turned out to be because inserts in large magazines were producing a lower 'hit rate' than the inserts previously placed in smaller magazines. The cause of this could have been at several levels:

1 The leaflets were wrongly designed for the type of magazine.
2 The wrong magazines were being used.

3 Inserts were no longer the best medium for recruiting supporters.

4 There are not that many people interested in new economics.

The further down the list, the more radical the revision to the strategy that would be required. Had the diagnosis been the last one, this might have led to a review of whether NEF should be a membership organisation at all. As it was, the cause was identified as inserts being the wrong medium, and the strategy for recruiting supporters has been changed.

Welsh Valleys Programme
Sometimes it may only be the way the target is expressed that needs changing. For instance, in Chapter 7 we gave the example of the Welsh Valleys Programme, aiming to reduce unemployment in the area by 25–30,000. The recession made this target unrealistic because jobs created by the programme were offset by jobs lost elsewhere. However, if the programme could still create 25–30,000 jobs in the recession, that, rather than the net effect, could become the target.

There is a note of caution that especially applies to voluntary organisations. Suppose that the indicators show that all or part of the strategy is off course. It may be possible to get back on course. But it may be that the strategy itself was misconceived. It is often difficult for voluntary organisations to abandon any part of their mission, because of their moral commitment to it. As Peter Drucker put it:

> Non-profit institutions generally find it impossible to abandon anything. Everything they do is 'the Lord's work' or 'a good cause'. But non-profits have to distinguish between moral causes and economic causes. A moral cause is an absolute good. Preachers have been thundering against fornication for five thousand years. Results, alas, have been nil, but that only proves how deeply entrenched evil is. The

absence of results indicates only that efforts have to be increased. This is the essence of a moral cause. In an economic cause, one asks: Is this the best application of our scarce resources?

As the hymn puts it, there is a time to live and a time to die. In Chapter 1 we said that it was possible that the result of strategy would be redundancy. The best way of sustaining the momentum may be to accept that an organisation's role is over, and for its members to put their energies into something else.

For example, one youth project could only continue to fund its centre by using funding from the Urban Programme to run schemes to remove young people from the unemployment register. Any young person who dropped into the centre was grabbed to do a job. The result was that they stopped using the centre. It might have been better if the project managers had accepted earlier on that their time was up.

Just as you should celebrate success, have a wake if part of your activities has to die.

The cycle

Most organisations will benefit from having an annual strategic planning cycle, just as they have an annual budgeting cycle. The results of one cycle provide input for the next cycle. But there is a big difference between planning and budgeting. The budgeting cycle frequently covers the same ground every year. This is unlikely to be true of the planning cycle, for several reasons.

To go through the whole cycle in detail each time may well induce strategy fatigue. People who may have invested enormous energy last time and who may still be involved in implementation may just not have any more energy to give.

It is also unnecessary, because unless the world is very turbulent most of the plan should stand from year to year. Table 5 gives a very approximate list of how long the different components of the plan should last:

Table 5 – Lifespan of the Plan

	Years
Vision	5 – 10
Mission and major goals	3 – 7
Written plan	2 – 5
Critical success factors	1 – 2

If we become too used to any activity, we cease to think about it and perform on 'automatic pilot'. Planning then becomes something to get through, irrespective of the results. So provide fresh stimulus by changing the process. Whether you have or have not used an outside facilitator, switch to the alternative.

Finally, the parts of the strategy and of the organisation that you want to concentrate upon will vary from year to year.

Example – focus of work on strategy

The New Economics Foundation (NEF) introduced strategic planning in 1988. The focus has been:

- 1988 – Mission and SWOT analysis
- 1989 – Reviewing the 1988 plan, since it was the first; defining the audience for NEF's activities
- 1990 – Linking activities to mission; structure; indicators
- 1991 – Root and branch review of everything with a consultant as facilitator
- 1992 – Fundraising and communication
- 1993 – As 1992, plus membership development and project development

Goodbye and good luck

This section is for those who have come to the end of this book, having gone through it for the first time. Here is an exercise to help you with your reactions.

Exercise 45   What stops you starting to plan?

Make a list of anything which stops you starting to plan tomorrow.

Possible obstacles are:

- lack of time
- lack of resources
- a feeling of being overwhelmed by technique
- a need for help
- too much conflict

All the points mentioned in the exercise are covered in this book:

- If time is short, set aside a day for the planning team to meet away from the office.
- Chapter 2 suggests where you might begin to look for resources. A strategic plan can itself be a great aid in fundraising.
- If technique seems overwhelming, investigate organisations similar to yours which have already tried strategic planning.
- If you want help, investigate what sources of help are available to you and consider using a consultant.
- Strategic planning can reduce conflict by providing an agreed sense of direction.

We hope that other worries are also covered.

So explain the benefits and the process of strategic planning to your colleagues. Take as many bites of the cherry as you need. Use this book and any other material you may have gathered. Pass the book and the material around. Try some of the exercises, especially those designed to help prepare the way for planning, such as numbers 1 and 40. There is a full list of the exercises on pages ix–x.

The benefits of planning are enormous – but the risks are large as well. Ultimately it is a question of whether you and your organisation believe the message of this book that the benefits outweigh the effort and the risks. This is a question of will: only your will can overcome the endless pressure to deal with short-term problems before thinking of the long term. There is a cautionary tale of a manager who joined an arts company that had received an award for its strategic planning. She said, 'When asked what my priorities would be I answered that producing a new three-year plan would be my first. The chair said, "Oh that can wait, it's more important to get the gents' toilet sorted out".' We hope that, armed with this book, you can make strategic planning such an inherent part of the running of your organisation that the question of doing one or the other never arises.

If you find that after reading the book you need to consolidate your understanding of the process as a whole, review Figure 2 on the stages of planning (page 19).

We would like to end with a case study which illustrates many of the points we have been making.

Case study: The New Economics Foundation

The New Economics Foundation (NEF) began life as an event, called The Other Economic Summit, or TOES. This was a conference held in London in 1984 to shadow the economic summit of the leaders of the seven leading industrial nations, known as the G7. NEF was set up in 1986 to provide a continuing organisation to promote the ideas developed in TOES.

In the first few years there was little formal strategy. This was for two reasons. Most activity was related to TOES. For example, a book called *The Living Economy* was produced from the papers presented to the first two conferences. There was also only one full-time employee, Paul Ekins, upon whose energy rested much of the success of TOES and the Foundation.

This phase came to an end when Paul left to become research director of the Right Livelihood Awards (the Alternative Nobel

Prize). Several of the original committee of management decided to step aside at about the same time. Duncan Smith, who was both a trustee and a member of the committee of management, took the lead in convening a meeting of the remaining committee of management and supporters of NEF who were interested in becoming more deeply involved. This became the executive committee. The change of name was a signal of intent that members become more actively involved. The new group agreed that it needed a formal strategy. A small 'action plan subcommittee' was set up to produce it.

The whole committee was deeply involved, as the following timetable, produced at the time, shows:

Date	Committee	Action plan subcommittee
19.2.88	Agreed on formal planning	
28.2.88		Prepared draft SWOT
By 7.3.88	Comments by individual members on SWOT plus suggestions for mission and key activities	
12.3.88		List of proposals for mission, key activities and revised SWOT
By 3.4.88	Key activities revised	
18.4.88		Provisional mission and key activities plus draft implementation plan
By 26.4.88	Further comments	
By 3.5.88		Plan revised
3.5.88	Plan presented to committee	
21.5.88	Plan presented to supporters' meeting	
1.7.88		Final version of plan
12.7.88	Plan distributed to all supporters	

This interactive process produced a great deal of consensus. A mission statement and SWOT were agreed without much difficulty. The mission statement was as follows:

> The New Economics Foundation exists to develop and promote a flexible economics which will lead to a high and sustainable quality of life for all.

The top three of each of the SWOT items were as follows:

Strengths
1 Unique in its holistic approach to the new economics.
2 Forum for a multi-disciplinary approach.
3 Links with other organisations.

Weaknesses
1 Lack of clarity created by different assumptions on what the new economics is.
2 Greater clarity on what the new economics is may divide the organisation.
3 Difficulty of raising core funding.

Opportunities
1 There are many who find conventional economics morally objectionable, unsatisfactory or difficult.
2 Changing climate suggests the time is ripe.
3 Few organisations active in individual fields of the new economic theory are concerned to educate the general public.

Threats
1 Economics seen as boring.
2 Economic roots of problems likely to be overlooked, causing our natural allies to steer clear of us.
3 Potential supporters may concentrate on small-scale local and individual projects and neglect the national and international dimensions.

A list of critical success factors produced by eight members of the committee showed varying levels of agreement:

Critical success factor	Number of people who included it in their list (maximum 8)
Funding	8
Publications programme	7
Closer relations with allies	5
Theoretical framework	5
Network of researchers	4
Director or spokesperson	3
Growing number of supporters	2
Practical initiatives	2

A couple of research studies were already in place, mainly as a result of the individual initiative of one person. NEF found further studies very difficult to fund. The two members of staff who had been recruited were fully occupied in servicing the committee and supporters. The best prospects for developing the new economics seemed to be a series of 12 working groups which were established at the supporters' meeting. These, however, quickly disintegrated, apart from one or two that had a great deal of support from the staff.

The analysis in the SWOT and CSFs was mostly sound, and the mission lasted, with a little alteration, for five years. It was, however, hugely ambitious for such a tiny organisation, despite an eminent list of patrons. The lack of experience meant that NEF found it impossible to plan for the resources needed to achieve the critical success factors. The fate of the working groups was one illustration of this.

In the circumstances, strategy was an uneasy mixture of deliberate and accidental. The unease was the result of a longstanding tension between two views of the organisation. The first was that NEF should be a think-tank with clear policies of its own. This would help with the lack of clarity identified as the main weakness above. It was also seen as essential if NEF was to become 'the media's first port of call when presented with alternative economic ideas'. The second, reflected in the second of the strengths above, was that NEF should be a forum or umbrella under which all those interested in developing a new economics could shelter. Those who took this view tended to worry about the second of the weaknesses listed above.

The mission statement sought to 'develop and promote' a new economics. Broadly speaking, the first view above reflected a preoccupation with promotion, and the second view with development. The consequence of the split was that 'accidental' successes tended not to be followed through and become emergent, since to do so would mean coming down on one or other side of the fence.

It took several years to understand that this was a 'both/and' issue, not an 'either/or'. The current approach is on the lines of a fried egg. The white is the umbrella, where ideas and proposals are given room to take shape and develop, whether through funded projects or simply through debate. The yolk is where ideas that have achieved consensus within the organisation are promoted to the outside world in whatever way seems best. The real issue is whether a particular idea should be in the white or in the yellow.

There were various related tensions, of which two stand out. Both were reflected in the fact that they were nominated as CSFs by only two or three people. First, the organisation had recruited almost 1,000 supporters. Some members of the committee wanted to treat them as a resource and to find ways of involving them much more. Others feared that they would become a distraction and that it was best to keep them at arm's length.

A second tension was the need for a director. Although an unsuccessful appeal in 1989 was intended to raise money for a director, there was at that point no consensus about the value of such a position.

Six-monthly reviews of strategy were introduced to provide space to debate these issues. The tensions continued, however, and a further element of frustration was introduced through the use of planning tools more formal than some members of the committee were comfortable with. (One of your co-authors has to plead guilty to this failure to ensure ownership!) The frustration showed in various comments on the third review of strategy, held in February 1990:

- 'The process should have been gone through, and a proper plan prepared, before the trustees were involved.'
- 'There was a limit to the amount we could plan, given that we had to react to new opportunities, such as Eastern Europe.'
- 'Would have preferred a more reflective process, and disliked the more mechanistic tools.'
- 'We had failed to achieve anything that would inspire our supporters.'

This period did see achievements. One of the research projects, for example, spawned in 1991 a book on *Alternative Economic Indicators* which became a bestseller in economics for its publisher, Routledge. A steady stream of books by supporters and sympathisers started to map out the new economics. 1991 also saw the return of TOES to London, with coverage in media ranging from Radio Bavaria to the *Caribbean Times*. Nevertheless, it all felt to those involved like swimming uphill through treacle. Just after TOES, indeed, one of the trustees wrote that, 'unless we can come up with some fresh approach which has a sharp cutting edge and focus, I cannot see any promising alternative either to limping along as we are at present or to winding up.'

It is always darkest just before the dawn. A review of strategy generated much more energy than hitherto. This was for several reasons:

- There was a felt need for it.
- Attendance was entirely voluntary.
- It was held away from London, at a convent in Kent.
- It lasted a whole weekend.
- It was facilitated for the first time by a consultant. His experience of the growing pains of other organisations was especially valuable.
- The agenda was extremely flexible.

Shortly afterwards, one of the trustees managed to raise core funding over three years. This doubled core income and enabled NEF to recruit a director. After several years' debate there was by now consensus on the need for a director. This in turn meant that there were the resources to do more than react. A deliberate strategy became feasible for the first time.

The new director was Ed Mayo, recruited from the World Development Movement. His initial strategy, which was adopted, was to concentrate on two areas: resources and communications. To provide resources, targets were set to double the number of supporters and to increase project funding. The former required further initiatives, such as investigating new methods of recruiting supporters and setting up a network of regional co-ordinators. The latter implied the need to develop NEF's understanding of and links with funders such as charitable trusts. Communications was an area long identified as important, but relatively neglected for lack of resources. Two themes were to be chosen each year to convey key messages. These messages were to be explicitly addressed to three core audiences in addition to supporters: non-governmental organisations, the media, and policy makers.

A year later, the strategy went deeper, in the sense of focusing on attributes rather than areas of work. These were credibility and capacity. Credibility was to be achieved particularly by building clusters of projects into programmes. The first two of these were on indicators and value based organisations. Capacity was to be achieved by identifying and acquiring the skills that were lacking. One example, reflected in the shift from projects to programmes, was the lack of co-ordination between projects.

The change over five years is shown by the 1993 set of CSFs:

- Perception of NEF's distinctive role and the quality of its work among target groups (eg measured by unsolicited comment)
- Staff satisfaction (eg expressed through appraisal process)
- Improved quality of project proposals (eg response from funders)

As Chapter 6 says, the fewer CSFs the better, so three is likely to be an improvement. Note also the attention to internal matters, in the form of staff satisfaction, and the measures attached to each CSF.

1993 therefore felt like the end of a cycle. Many of the original issues and tensions had been explored and dealt with. A series of new issues was starting to appear. Accountability was one – if NEF was unsure who its audiences and its stakeholders were, to whom should it make itself accountable? A second was the management of growth – there were up to 15 people working in two small rooms. It felt like time to rewrite the mission, to make it less all-embracing and more specific. The director was seen reading chapter four of this book . . .

Appendix 1
Techniques

Techniques are mentioned at various points in the book where they are particularly relevant. However, there are some techniques that may come in useful at several stages during planning.

Techniques for generating ideas

Note that techniques for generating ideas are separate from techniques for evaluating ideas. If the two are combined, the evaluation will inhibit creativity and reduce the number of ideas generated.

Brainstorming

- Especially if the technique is unfamiliar, you may want to have a warm-up session. This usually seems to involve brainstorming the uses of a paperclip, but anything will do.
- The leader of the session defines the problem and restates it: 'In how many ways can we . . .'
- Participants call out ideas as they think of them. The leader writes them up on a flipchart. The more ideas the better. No comments are allowed on ideas, except to clarify what they mean.
- Allow 15–40 minutes for the brainstorming session.

Brainwriting

This is similar to brainstorming, except that everyone writes their ideas down. One variation is to swap sheets when you have run out of ideas so that you are stimulated by the ideas of others. Another variation is to have different sheets marked with different themes (eg different services that the organisation might offer), and for everyone to put their ideas on each sheet in turn.

Stimulating additional ideas

Whether you are using brainstorming or brainwriting, there are ways to stimulate extra ideas. Here are two examples.

Variations on a theme

Look at all the variations on a theme. Suppose you are thinking of starting a toy library for the under-5s. You could look at lending the under-5s objects other than toys. You could look at lending to the over-5s. You could look at using toys for purposes other than lending, eg for play sessions. And so on.

Metaphors

Someone produces, at random, a metaphor for the issue you are concerned with. 'This organisation is like a doughnut', for example. You then brainstorm or write down all the ways in which this might be true. You then choose another metaphor and repeat the process. This approach shifts people away from their preconceptions and provides new angles. Velcro fasteners are said to have been developed in this way.

Techniques for evaluating ideas

The simplest technique is just to list the ideas generated and discuss them as a group. Below are some further suggestions.

Snowball

Members of the group are asked to write each of their ideas on a separate Post-It note and to stick the note on a wall, next to similar ideas. As a second stage, they are asked to suggest labels for groups of notes and to shift notes between groups if they think it appropriate. The pattern usually stabilises by itself. If it does not, a point of difference will have emerged which is equally valuable.

Ranking

Sometimes a rank order of ideas is needed, eg so that the most important idea is tackled first. A simple ranking can be carried out in a group, or it can be done individually and the results combined.

Paired comparisons

When there are relatively few ideas to evaluate, each separate pair of ideas can be compared. For example, if your organisation has five main strengths, a paired comparison can show the cause and effect relationships between them. This is best done in a group.

Q-sort

A Q-sort is useful when there is a large number of ideas (say more than 30), which can be difficult to rank directly. First the most important idea is identified, then the least important, then the most important idea remaining, then the least important idea remaining, and so on. This too is best done in a group.

Force field analysis

Force field analysis is a way of mapping the forces for and against a particular change. By bringing them out into the open the analysis can show ways of tackling situations where progress seemed impossible.

1 *Define the change you want to see.* Define the problem, a present position with which you are dissatisfied, as concretely as possible. This can be hard, since problems are often not what they first seem. Then define the position that you want to reach, representing the solution. A gap analysis (see page 80) may help.

2 *List the forces for and against the change.*
- These forces are not just people – they may be structures, processes or features of the culture.
- Be precise. You may, for example, find that a force seems to be both for and against. This means that it has to be separated into its component parts, some of which will be for, others against.
- Identify any irresistible forces or immovable objects that can by themselves make the change happen, or stop it happening.
- Rate each force as 'strong', 'medium' or 'weak'.
- Try to understand why each force is for or against, and why it has the strength it has.

3 *Draw the forces on a diagram.*

For the change

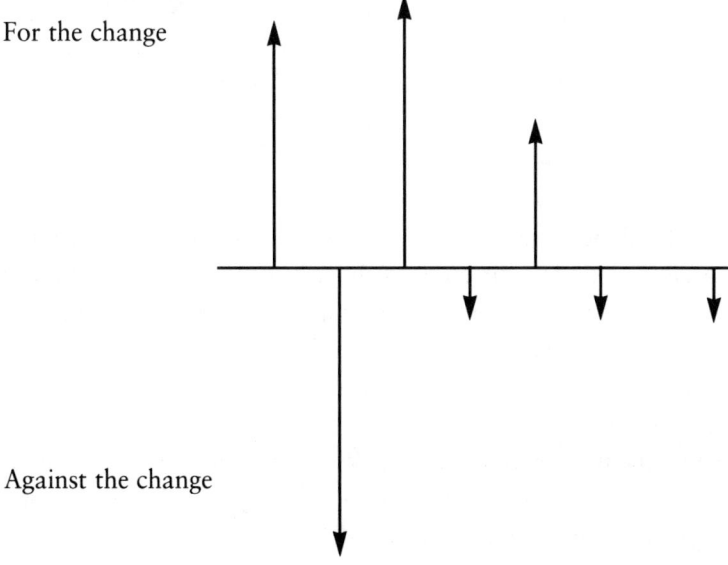

Against the change

- The length of each force should be in proportion to its impact.
- Draw irresistible forces or immovable objects as thick lines.
- If the forces can be grouped, there is an alternative way of drawing the diagram:

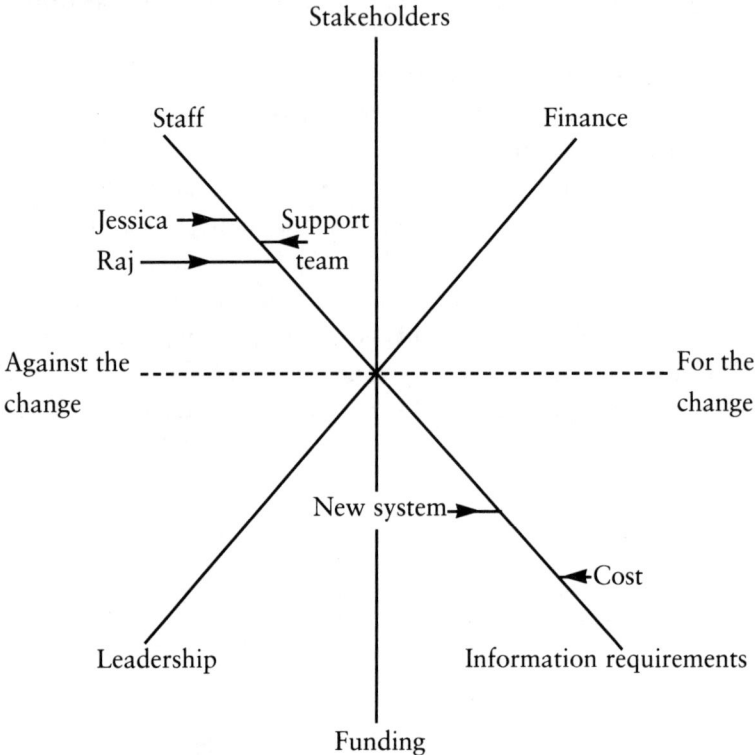

- Label all the forces – in this example, only a few of the forces have been named. The direction of the arrow shows whether they are for or against the change. Those for could be in one colour, those against in another.

4 *Using the diagram.*
- Does the balance of forces suggest that the change is possible?
- Which forces for change can be strengthened? Which forces against change can be weakened?

Decision-making processes

Strategic planning develops an excitement and a momentum in the organisation. The danger of this is that people get carried away and choose strategies without proper thought. Here are two methods for avoiding the danger.

Devil's advocacy

When there is a proposal on the table, a possible check on whether it has been thought through is for someone to argue the case for not pursuing it, whether or not that is his or her real opinion.

Dialectical enquiry

A similar approach is to develop opposing recommendations, and for different groups to argue the merits of each.

Appendix 2
Glossary

Benchmarking Learning from best practice in other organisations.

Consumer/user value chain The sequence or chain of activities that together deliver the value of the service or product.

Critical success factor A factor vital to success.

Culture In an organisation, the mixture of values, attitudes and behaviour that makes up 'the way we do things around here'.

Evaluation Reviewing the process of planning in order to learn for the next round.

Experience curve Relates the level of experience of doing something to the efficiency with which it is done.

Gap analysis Analysis of the gap between the present and the desired position.

Goals A specific objective (qv). There is usually a timescale for achievement. Achievement is usually capable of being measured.

Indicators Measures (qv) of performance that can be quantified.

Input Resources committed to an activity.

Life cycle The cycle from birth through development and maturity to death. Applies to concepts and services as well as living things.

Measures Gauges of performance that may be either quantitative or qualitative.

Mission The reason for the existence of the organisation.

Monitoring The collection and analysis of information.

Objectives An end that contributes to the mission.

Organisational capability An organisation's will and capacity to act.

Outcome The impact of an activity on an organisation's goals or objectives.

Output The results or consequences of an activity.

PEST A framework for appraising an organisation's external environment. The acronym stands for political, economic, social and technological.

Portfolio analysis A comparative evaluation of an organisation's portfolio (or range) of activities.

Scenario A picture of a possible future.

Stakeholder Anybody with an interest or stake in the organisation.

Strategic planning The process of developing strategy.

Strategy How an organisation interacts with its environment and changes internally to achieve its purpose.

Structure The formal arrangement of activities and functions, and the relationship between them.

SWOT An acronym for the examination of strengths, weaknesses, opportunities and threats.

Values Underlying beliefs.

Appendix 3
Useful Addresses

The Management Development Team at NCVO maintains information on suitable consultants and trainers. It can be contacted at

> NCVO
> Regent's Wharf
> 8 All Saints Street
> London N1 9RL
> Tel: 071-713 6161
> Fax: 071-713 6300

Hilary Barnard and Perry Walker collaborate as consultants in helping voluntary organisations with their strategic planning. They can be contacted at

> 214 Richmond Road
> London E8 3QN
> Tel and fax: 071-241 3328

Appendix 4
References and Recommended Reading

Meredith Belbin, *Management Teams: Why they Succeed or Fail,* Heinemann, 1981

Cliff Bowman and David Asch, *Strategic Management,* Macmillan, 1987 – a good leading general text on strategy

John Bryson, *Strategic Planning for Public and Not For Profit Organisations,* Jossey Bass, 1988 – an excellent pioneering book in the field

Richard J Butler and David C Wilson, *Managing Voluntary and Non Profit Organizations,* Routledge, 1990

Peter Drucker, *Managing the Non-Profit Organisation,* Butterworth-Heinemann, 1990

Dina Glouberman, *Life Choices and Life Changes Through Imagework: The Arts of Developing Personal Vision,* Unwin, 1989 – a good aid for work on developing vision

Charles Handy, *Understanding Organizations,* Penguin, 1985 – an approachable introductory book

Charles Handy, *Understanding Voluntary Organizations,* Penguin, 1988

Gerry Johnson and Kevan Scholes, *Exploring Corporate Strategy,* Prentice Hall, 1993 – the UK and European bestseller on strategy, now in its third edition; a good general text on strategy

Henry Mintzberg, *Structure in Fives,* Prentice Hall, 1983 – a more advanced book on organisational structure

Henry Mintzberg and A McHugh, 'Strategy formation in an adhocracy', *Administrative Science Quarterly*, vol 30, no 2, pp 167–97 – core ideas on emergent strategy

Rosabeth Moss Kanter, *The Change Masters*, Unwin, 1984 – contains much of interest on managing change

NCVO, *On Trust*, NCVO, 1992

Paul Nutt and Robert Backoff, *Strategic Management of Public and Third Sector Organisations*, Jossey Bass, 1992

Open University, *Strategic Management* course workbooks, B881 course, 1989

Michael Porter, *Competitive Advantage*, Free Press, 1985 – key source for private sector value chain analysis

Rick Rogers, *Using Consultants*, NCVO, 1992

Peter Senge, *The Fifth Discipline: The Art & Practice of The Learning Organization*, Century Business, 1992

Alvin Toffler, 'The Art of Measuring The Arts', *The Annals of the American Academy*, 1966, pp 141–155

Appendix 5
Comments Sheet

This sheet has been included to enable readers to feed back their experience, and to suggest ways in which the book could be improved.

Name:

Organisation:

Address and phone number:

- Which parts of the book have you found most helpful and why?

- Which parts of the book have you found most difficult and why?

- Which parts of the book have you found most difficult to use?

- Which parts of the book would you like to see expanded?

- What gaps are there in this book that you would like to see filled?

- What changes has using this book led to in your organisation?

- Can you provide examples of strategic planning at work in your organisation (eg strategic plans, documents setting out the process, critical success factors etc)?

Please return this comments sheet to Hilary Barnard and Perry Walker, 214 Richmond Road, London E8 3QN

Index

Index